100 CREATIVE Activities for Sabbath

Karen Holford

Pacific Press® Publishing Association
Nampa, Idaho
Oshawa, Ontario, Canada
www.pacificpress.com

Designed by Linda Griffith

Additional copies of this book are available by calling toll free 1-800-765-6955
or visiting http://www.adventistbookcenter.com.

Library of Congress Cataloging-in-Publication Data

Holford, Karen.
100 creative activities for sabbath / Karen Holford.
p. cm.
ISBN: 0-8163-2139-6
ISBN 13: 9780816321391
1.Sabbath 2. Family—Religious life. 3. Seventh-day Adventists—Doctrines.
I. Title: One hundred creative activities for Sabbath. II. Title.

BX6154.H577 2006
263'.2—dc22   2005058692

06 07 08 09 10 • 5 4 3 2 1

Dedication

To
Bethany, Nathan, and Joel
with love

OTHER BOOKS BY KAREN HOLFORD

Danger at Deerwood Grove

The Family Book

I Miss Grandpa

The Loneliest Grief

Muddy Fingers, Sticky Feet

100 Creative Prayer Ideas for Kids

100 Quick and Easy Worship Ideas for Kids

Contents

Wordless Scriptures
Letters From the Bible
Refreshed Parables
Scripture Sculptures
Creative Characters
God's Names
Rainbow Promise Books
Scripture Calligraphy
Bible Scenes

Spiritual Family Tree
Answered-Prayer Stories
Spiritual-Gift Boxes
Dream, Help, Love, Smile
Family Altars
Family Advertisements
Thank-You Cards
Family Blessings
Family Life Journeys
Family-Faith Collage

Spiritual Scrapbooking
Creating Cards
Christian Craft Projects for Children
Creating Mini-books
Making Puppets
Creating a City of God
Creating Witness T-Shirts
Sabbath Candle Lanterns
Bible-Promise Boxes
Ready-Made Bible Crafts

Musical Scriptures
The Hum Game
Write Your Own Praise Song
Scrapbook of Songs
Making Your Own Instruments
Hymn and Song Stories
Musical Mimes
Sound Scriptures
Christian Drama
Illustrated Songs

Preface

A MESSAGE FOR PARENTS

The seventh-day Sabbath is very significant for Adventists. It identifies us as being different from many other Christians. It is also a special part of our heritage and something we want our children to treasure all their lives.

Today, our surroundings and circumstances are often very different from the world in which we grew up, and even more different from the world in which our parents were reared. Sabbath preparation is more challenging when both parents work full time outside the home or commute long distances. In a multimedia world, children have come to expect high-quality, vibrant entertainment. Many of us live in cities and don't have the opportunity to enjoy the countryside, surrounded by plants and animals. Some of us don't have our own cars and have to depend on public transport to get to and from church. Some of us live in communities where being street-wise is a matter of survival.

This book is designed to provide a variety of activities for twenty-first-century families living in a wide range of circumstances. Many of the traditional "countryside" Sabbath activities are not readily available to a family that lives in a small apartment block in a large city and has no car. Choose the activities to suit your needs, your child's interests, and the Sabbath culture with which you are comfortable. Adapt the activities and be flexible with them. Take the basic ideas and make them your own. But most of all, keep in mind God's plans for your Sabbaths, and ensure that you are creating special memories for your children. Sabbaths need to be happy and interesting days during which children can learn about God's creation and His love and relax together with happy families and friends.

The first key to happy Sabbaths is careful planning. Choose Sabbath activities at least a week in advance and check that you have everything you need for the activity to run smoothly. The second key to happy Sabbaths is knowing how to excite your child about the activity you have planned. The third key is making whatever happens enjoyable. You can't plan everything to perfection, but make the most of teachable moments, and just enjoy being with your child as you discover more about God's love and His creation.

Most of the ideas in this book have been designed to be used by mixed groups of adults, children, and teenagers, because families include peoples of all ages.

I pray that this book will enrich your Sabbaths, bring you closer to God and to each other, and create memories for your family that will strengthen your faith and commitment to God.

Karen Holford
September 2005

Introduction

WHAT'S SABBATH ALL ABOUT?

Genesis 2:2, 3

Here we read that Sabbath was designed to commemorate God's week of Creation. In many ways Sabbath is a celebration of Creation and the amazing creative power of God. We are invited to explore the diversity of God's creativity and to be filled with wonder at all He has made. We can also use our God-given creativity to explore our relationship with God and with each other, and to use our creative skills to worship God and share His love with others. The Sabbath is also a day of rest. Even though God didn't need to rest, He knew we would, and He knew we needed a day to pause and reconnect with Him and with each other, in a relaxed time and space, protected from our busy weekly schedules.

Exodus 20:8–11

What a gift! A day when we have permission not to work! Sabbath is a day to rest, to pause, and to allow our minds and bodies to do something different from what we would usually do during the other days of the week. Sabbath is also a day to be with our families and other people living in our communities. The Sabbath day has been especially blessed by God for us. How can we be more aware of all the blessings that God has carefully provided for us in the Sabbath?

Isaiah 58:13, 14

The Sabbath is to be a delight, not a drudgery. A celebration of our spirituality rather than a day of restrictions. It is a time to pause from the usual business of our lives. It is also a day to be respected and kept holy, where we consciously choose to do things that preserve the sanctity of the Sabbath.

Matthew 12:1–13

The Sabbath is a day to share the love of Jesus with others and to bring them hope and healing. The Sabbath is a gift from God for human beings: It was made especially for us, and we are not to destroy its beauty by filling it with human restrictions, as the Pharisees tried to do.

The Sabbath was made as a gift for human beings!
It is a day to rest from our work.
- A day to worship God
- A day to grow closer to God and learn more about Him
- A day to grow closer to each other as families and friends

- A day to discover the delights of God's creation
- A day to explore the Bible
- A day to share God's love with others
- A day to celebrate being a child of God

IDEAS FOR SIMPLE SABBATH CELEBRATIONS

One of the best tips for creating a happy Sabbath atmosphere in the home is to plan ahead so that everything is ready and you can relax together. By making Sabbath attractive and appealing to the senses, you are helping your child to create strong memories of special family times, treats, and celebrations. You can explain to your child that you use the candles and fragrances, etc., as reminders that God has made the Sabbath as a special gift for us.

You could invite your child to help you choose the food for Sabbath lunch. If you have more than one child, they could take turns choosing the beverage, the main course, and the dessert. If you decide on the Sabbath menu on Sunday, you can prepare ahead and freeze the food. Or take your child to the store and let him or her choose pre-prepared food for Sabbath to reduce your workload.

Add special touches to a Sabbath table. Your child could design and draw some Sabbath placemats that you could laminate and reuse each Sabbath. Light some special candles, or use tea-light holders and tea-lights as a low-cost alternative to fancy candles. Tea-lights can look lovely in a simple glass, resting in sand or even salt to prevent the heat from the tea-light cracking the glass. Place a single fresh flower on the table, in a tall glass tied with raffia or wired ribbon.

Add fragrance to Sabbath by using scented tea-lights, by simmering spices on the stove, or by baking your own bread or using ready-to-bake bread dough.

As a special treat, your child might like to use a light stick to welcome the Sabbath. Light sticks are plastic sticks that light when you "crack" them. The crack allows chemicals to mix, which then produce a neon-type glow for a few hours. The stick can usually be bent to create a circle to slip on a child's wrist or around a glass.

Some families have special pillows, a throw for a sofa, or a different tablecloth, which add a Sabbath touch to their homes.

Some Jewish families hold "Welcome Sabbath!" parties on Friday evening during which the Sabbath is enthusiastically and energetically welcomed. How could you welcome the Sabbath with exuberance in your home?

Find ways to honor and bless each other as part of the Sabbath routine in your home. You could ask each person to share the best and worst thing that happened in the week. Celebrate with the good things that happened and offer comfort and concern for the challenging things. When you close Sabbath on Saturday evening, you could talk together about your hopes and fears for the next week so that you can pray for each other during the week ahead.

Invite your child to share ideas about ways to celebrate your Sabbaths together. Above all, aim to create beautiful memories that will last a lifetime, as these memories will guide them in their spiritual journeys, wherever they decide to go.

IDEAS FOR SERMON-FOCUSED ACTIVITIES DURING
THE CHURCH SERVICE

Here are some ideas to help engage your child with the sermon.

Draw a series of simple pictures to illustrate the sermon while the pastor is preaching. These don't have to be artistic, just simple and symbolic, using stick people. Add written comments that help make the sermon theme accessible and relevant to your child. In the end you will have a simple "comic strip" of the sermon. You could collect these and keep them in a folder. As your child grows up, he might like to create his own illustrated sermons to show you over Sabbath lunch or to help him focus on the sermon themes.

If you know the theme of the sermon, you may be able to find a Bible storybook that tells the same story in a style that is more accessible to your child. This is easier if your pastor is doing a series on Bible characters or parables, or other topics that storybooks cover.

Invite your child to rewrite the Scripture reading in her own words, or to write it as a rhyming poem or comic strip with illustrations.

Using graph paper, invite your child to create a crossword from the words the pastor is using in his sermon, adding extra words to the crossword as the sermon progresses.

Suggest that your child create a poster to advertise the theme of the sermon on a church bulletin board, or to be hung outside the church to introduce the idea of the sermon to passersby in a way that would make them stop and think.

Give your child a notebook to record any stories or sermon illustrations that pastors tell during their sermons. They can keep the notebook and add more stories to it from week to week.

If your pastor is preaching a sermon that is hard for your child to relate to, suggest that she read a chapter of Proverbs from a modern translation and draw cartoons to illustrate each proverb or find and illustrate the funniest proverb in the chapter.

Adults usually take away only one useful thought from a sermon. Help your child to find the one thought he would like to take away from each sermon and to write the thought on a bulletin board at home or in a notebook that is kept for recording these ideas.

Take the theme of the sermon and create your own mini-challenge for your child. For example, if the sermon is about marriage, you could ask your child to write a list of qualities she would look for in a Christian spouse. Keep the list—and surprise her at her wedding!

HOW YOUR CHURCH CAN HELP FAMILIES CELEBRATE SABBATH

Expand the church library to create a special Sabbath activity library that includes Sabbath/Bible games and jigsaw puzzles, videos suitable for Sabbath, and interesting books for children of all ages.

Start a special family Sabbath club, where families can come and participate in a Sabbath activity together. Families in a church can take turns organizing a Sabbath treasure hunt, Sabbath craft activity, Bible game, or one of the many different ideas in this book. This shares the burden of planning for activities and enables busy families to find the time to celebrate Sabbath more creatively.

If you worship in a city, other Adventist churches may be nearby. The Sabbath club could be shared among a group of churches, or each church could publish a list of the Sabbath programs happening in other churches so that families can have a wider choice of Sabbath afternoon and evening programs to attend.

If your church has regular Sabbath afternoon programs, evaluate how they contribute to family togetherness on Sabbath. Does the programming give space for families to do things together? How are the children experiencing the programs? What else could be done during these programs so that children and families experience Sabbath as a spiritual and relational delight?

If you have weekly Sabbath afternoon programs, consider leaving one week a month without any program, and encourage families and groups of singles to try one of the activities in this book or to plan their own Sabbath activity. Then organize a program during which families can share their ideas and how they worked out to inspire each other.

Start a folder of ideas for Sabbath activities in your city or area. Invite families to contribute ideas about their favorite Sabbath activities, walks, places to visit, and crafts, etc. Families can also contribute any special Bible treasure hunts or trails that they have developed. These ideas could also be added to your church's Web site or published in your church's newsletter or bulletin.

CREATING A SABBATH BACKPACK

This is a list of things that may be worth including in your Sabbath backpack. If you keep the bag well stocked, it will be ready and waiting for you when you need it:

- Small Bible
- Small pocket-sized Bible concordance
- Notebooks or pads of paper or plain index cards
- Pens, pencils, crayons, erasers, etc.
- Clipboards for writing and drawing when there are no tables to use
- Magnifying glass
- Binoculars
- Plastic-backed blanket or something to sit on

- Small cartons of juice or bottles of water
- Sunscreen
- Healthful fruit and cereal snack bars
- Self-sealing plastic bags for special discoveries
- Cleansing hand wipes or antibacterial gel
- Small first-aid kit
- Tissues
- Umbrella
- Camera, preferably digital
- Any extra clothing that may be needed
- A disposable tablecloth to cover a picnic table and create a clean surface
- Money for emergencies

SECTION I

Outdoor Activities

CHAPTER I

City Walks

Even in the city streets, there are different things we can look for and do that will focus our minds on Jesus. God is as present in the town or city as He is in the countryside, but we may need to look at our environment in a new way to see Him there.

The city is full of people, and Jesus went where the people were and loved them. As you travel around your town on Sabbath, look out for the people whom Jesus would have noticed, and think how you could show them something of Jesus' love.

- Bible-Verse Word Hunts
- Search Light
- Cross Hunt
- Posters for Jesus
- Hidden Parables
- Prayer Walking
- Treasure Hunt
- Love Detectives
- Street-Name Puzzle
- Sidewalk Chalk

1

Bible-Verse Word Hunts

This activity is a kind of treasure hunt that you can do almost instantly during a city walk. It can also be an unusual way to help you memorize a Bible verse.

THINGS YOU NEED:

- Bible
- Pencil
- Paper
- Clipboard
- Camera (optional)

What you do:

1. As a family, choose a Bible verse that does not have too many unusual words. Write the verse clearly down the side of a piece of paper, with one word per line.
2. Clip the paper to the clipboard and take a pen or pencil with you.
3. As you walk, watch for any words that are in your chosen Bible verse. You might find the words almost anywhere, such as on signs, posters, street names, stores, or cafes. Look in unusual places, such as above eye-level, where there might be commemorative plaques or even graffiti. Perhaps you might see a word on a taxi, truck, car, or store bag.
4. When you find a word in your verse, describe where you found it on the line next to the word.
5. See how much of the verse you can find together.

Other ideas:

- Photograph each of the words in the location where you found them. When you get home, make a verse collage by downloading the photos to your computer and cropping and rearranging them to make an unusual poster of the verse.
- Give each person a different Bible verse of a similar length and see who can complete their verse first.
- If you are having a Sabbath at home, use a magazine or newspaper to search for the words in your verse. Tear out the words and glue them to a sheet of paper to make a verse collage. Decorate the verse with appropriate pictures and motifs that you found in the newspaper. If you do not wish to use secular magazines for this activity, use discarded church papers and magazines.

2

Search Light

Jesus said that He is the Light of the world (see John 8:12). Today our world contains all kinds of lights. This activity invites us to explore some of the various aspects of Jesus inspired by some of the different lights around us.

THINGS YOU NEED:

- Pencil
- Paper
- Clipboard

What you do:

1. As you go for a walk, look for the different lights around you, such as a street light, car light, road crossing light, light on an ambulance, decorative lights, advertising lights, and warning lights.
2. When you find a light, stop and discuss what that particular light tells you about Jesus as the Light of the world. Even small children can have ideas that they can be encouraged to share, or they can draw the lights that you find.
3. Write down your ideas or record your conversations so you can listen to them later.
4. Perhaps you could also photograph the lights and place the pictures in an album. Write down your insights about Jesus as the Light of the world and glue these thoughts around the photos.
5. Discuss questions like these: What kinds of light are we as we shine in our work, school, home, and community? How can we make sure that our lights shine effectively?

Another idea:

- This idea could be developed to become the basis of a sermon or devotional. The photographed lights and the insights you shared could be combined to make a PowerPoint presentation.

3

Cross Hunt

God is with us wherever we are. One way to remind ourselves that God is always near is to look for any cross shapes we can find that were not originally designed to be crosses. You may be surprised at how many you can find! The great news is that these crosses are all empty! Jesus is now in heaven and has given us the amazing gift of salvation!

THINGS YOU NEED:

- Pencil
- Paper
- Clipboard
- Camera (optional)

What you do:

1. As you walk, look around you for cross shapes. For example, the bars in a window often contain a cross shape, as well as the pattern in paving slabs on the ground, brickwork, railings, fences, etc. Small children can also be involved in the hunt.
2. Write down all the places where you found a cross shape. Try to find them in as many different places as you can. How many different ones can you find in a short walk? How can you become more aware of God's presence with you at all times and in all places?
3. You could photograph the crosses you find and make a poster of cross shapes.
4. Every time you see a cross, remember how much God loves you!

Another idea:

- Instead of looking for a cross, choose another shape. This may be harder! Consider looking for hearts or Christian fish symbols.

4

Posters for Jesus

When you walk through a city, you can usually see many posters advertising all kinds of things. When you see a poster on Sabbath, you might like to try this activity.

THINGS YOU NEED:

- Pencil
- Paper
- Clipboard
- Marker pens
- Camera (optional)

What you do:

1. Find a place where there are several posters advertising different kinds of products. Study them to see if any of them could be adapted to make good advertisements for Jesus, the Christian life, prayer, or Christian character qualities.
2. Redesign them on your paper so that they advertise Jesus instead of cereal or laundry detergent, etc.
3. Show your ideas to each other.
4. Discuss questions like these: What might your new posters tell people in your community about Jesus? How do we advertise Jesus in our lives and in our community? What characteristics of Jesus would you most want to feature if you were His publicity agent? How can we use some of the best of commercial advertising concepts to promote the most important things about our faith and God's love?

Other ideas:

- If you can't get outside, select a few advertisements from a magazine and give one to each person. How could they be adapted to advertise Jesus?
- If you enjoy working with computers, scanners, and graphics, you could create and print your own new version of the poster.
- Instead of creating posters to advertise Jesus, use the advertisements to inspire mini-drama commercials that advertise Jesus.
- If you are in a large group, divide into smaller groups to design a T-shirt, poster, TV-style commercial, or other advertising product to promote Jesus, Christianity, grace, or other Christian themes. Share your ideas at the end of the activity by showing your designed advertising products and talking about them.
- Perhaps you could print one of the ideas as a large poster to be placed outside your church.
- You might like to look at the Christian Publicity Organization's Web site <www.cpo-online.org.uk> and catalogue for some creative poster ideas.

5

Hidden Parables

Jesus used the everyday stories of making bread, working, caring for sheep, and farming when He told His parables two thousand years ago. What stories might He tell if He came to your city today? What local stories might He use for inspiration? What everyday activities might He use for His parables?

THINGS YOU NEED:
- Pencil
- Notebook for recording your ideas

What you do:

All you need to do for this activity is to walk around your city, looking for object lessons or parables in the normal and everyday events of city life. Take a walk together and point out possible parables as you notice them. Or sit down at the end of the walk, in a park or at home, and share the parables you have discovered.

Examples:
- The parable of the lost subway pass that the senior citizen lost in her home. She swept and cleaned until she found it. Then she went out to meet her friends and to celebrate finding her pass.
- The kingdom of God is like a subway train. It will go on its journey, but you have to choose whether or not to get on the train.
- The parable of the persistent weed that kept trying to find a crack in the concrete until it could emerge into the light and grow.

Other ideas:
- Write the contemporary parables in a notebook and add to them when you think of more. Add photos and other items to illustrate the stories.
- Use the parables to inspire mimes, skits, and songs to be performed in church or at a youth or outreach program.

6

Prayer Walking

There are so many people in a city with so many needs. At times it can seem overwhelming. How can a few Christians make a difference in a busy city? Jonah was one man, but he made a huge difference in Nineveh. Christians can still make a big difference because we have access to prayer and to God.

THINGS YOU NEED:

- Pencil
- Paper or notebook for recording prayer needs and requests

What you do:

1. First, come together as a family or group and pray for your neighborhood, street, or apartment block. Pray that God will open your eyes, ears, and hearts to the spiritual, physical, and emotional needs of those around you.
2. Then, quietly and reverently, go for a walk. As you pass each building or apartment, pray for the people who live, work, or study there. Watch for clues that may offer you hints for your prayers, such as toys that show that children may live there, ramps that show that a disabled person might live there, lots of bottles outside that may indicate someone with an alcohol problem lives there, or signs of poverty and hardship.
3. Pray silently as you pass the buildings and jot down any house numbers and notes that you especially want to remember.
4. When you finish your walk, discuss what you noticed and how it felt to pray for your neighborhood in this way.

Other ideas:

- Repeat this prayer walk whenever you can, especially around the same streets and homes. You may never know until heaven how your prayers changed the lives of the people in your neighborhood.
- Become acquainted with some of the people along your prayer walk if you see them on the doorstep or in their yards.
- Organize your church community to become prayer sponsors for an area of your city. Members could prayer walk the streets together, if it is safe to do so, and even shut-in members can be given a street to pray for.
- Perhaps your city has open census data and electoral information that lists the names of people living at various addresses. If so, copies of this information can help you pray for people by name.

Treasure Hunt

This activity takes some extra planning and effort, but it can be worth the time it takes to produce an interesting treasure hunt in your area.

THINGS YOU NEED:
- Map of the area
- Notebook
- Pencil
- Digital camera (optional)

What you do:

1. Shortly before you plan to hold this treasure hunt, take the time to research the area where you will hold the hunt. If possible, choose an attractive and historic part of the town. Walk slowly up and down the streets, looking out for all kinds of interesting details that could be woven into a Sabbath treasure hunt. Look for items that may have connections with Bible stories or are connected to local people who did great things. Look out for words on buildings and even on the lampposts and drain covers. Try to notice things that often get overlooked. Carefully write down all the details of the things that could be useful to your treasure hunt.

2. When you have lots of material, sit down and work out your clues and how you will organize the hunt. Think about the ages and the abilities of the people who will be doing the hunting. You will probably want to accompany them, so you will be around if they get into difficulties or miss something.

3. You can include directions in your treasure hunt, telling the hunters where to turn left and right, cross roads, and other specific instructions. Or you can mark off a small area on a map and explain that all the clues will be inside those boundaries. Or you can scramble the names of the streets and list the clues that can be found in each street under the scrambled name and let the hunters work out their own route.

4. Try to keep the clues connected with the Bible and nature and true stories about local people.

5. Decide how you want the hunt to end—at a specific place or when they have discovered all the clues. What will the treasure be? A picnic, perhaps, or some items from a Christian book store?

Other ideas:

- If this treasure hunt works well, share it with other families in your church so that they can enjoy it too. Maybe they could do a treasure hunt in another part of town and you could swap with them.

8

Love Detectives

God's love is everywhere. We just need to open our eyes to look for it! This activity helps us to develop detective skills for tracking down signs of God's love all around us.

THINGS YOU NEED:
- Notebooks
- Pencils
- Self-sealing plastic bags for collecting removable evidence
- Magnifying glass and binoculars (optional)
- Camera (optional)

What you do:
1. Explain to your children that they are going to become detectives. This is a fun idea for most children!
2. Take them out for a walk and ask them to hunt for any clues they can find that show that God is love.
3. They have to move silently and quietly and jot down ideas in their notebooks.
4. If they get stuck and can't find any clues of their own, offer them some of your ideas to get them started. Perhaps they can find an exquisite flower growing through the sidewalk, showing that beautiful created things can still grow in the city. Perhaps they will notice someone helping another person and showing them love. Perhaps they can feel the warmth of the sunshine that reminds them of the warmth of God's love.
5. You may like to use the camera to take pictures of your evidence and to keep a box of any collectable evidence of God's love that you can find.

Other ideas:
- If you can access a tall building with a safe rooftop and a good view, try doing this activity from way up high as you look down on the city. The binoculars will be very useful here!
- Have a church project in which people bring photos, items, or other evidence of God's love to display and talk about as a kind of show-and-tell program.

9

Street-Name Puzzle

This is a puzzle that may take a little while for you to create, but it can be another way of giving a city walk a Sabbath twist.

THINGS YOU NEED:

- Bible
- Map of the area where you will be walking
- Pen
- Paper

What you do:

1. Choose a Bible verse that is not too long.
2. Write the verse vertically down the middle of your piece of paper, with one letter per line. You may need more than one piece of paper.
3. Then, write local street names horizontally across the paper so that one letter of the street name is also one letter of the Bible verse.
4. Create some simple clues for the street names or for the things that might only be found in that street.
5. Rewrite the puzzle without the street names, but with one underlined space per letter of the street name, with the underlined letters of the Bible text letters highlighted in a different color and vertically underneath each other.
6. When you go for a walk, give your family the street clue sheet with the underlined spaces, and let them collect the answers as you walk together. Slowly the Bible verse will be revealed.

For example:

This street is where your school is	A N **G** E L R O A D
This street has a yellow building	F L **O** W E R S T R E E T
Mrs. Francis lives here	**D** U T C H Q U A R T E R

The highlighted letters spell **God.**

Other ideas:

- Look in Bible puzzle books for other puzzle ideas. One kind of puzzle places numbers under some of the letters in the answers to its questions. When the numbered letters are put in the correct order, they will spell out a Bible verse.

For example:

This street is where your school is	A N G E L R O A D
This would also spell **God.**	1 2 3

10

Sidewalk Chalk

In some cities, sidewalk or pavement artists are quite popular. Perhaps you and your family or group could try creating some witnessing art on a spare piece of pavement. Check if there are any regulations about where you can do this, so that you do not cause an obstruction. It may be preferable to do this activity in a park, instead, where there may be more space.

THINGS YOU NEED:

• Sidewalk chalk

For ideas on what you can draw on the sidewalk, you might like to explore the Internet for designs used on Christian witness T-shirts, etc., to stimulate your creativity: <www.religioustshirts.co.uk>.

What you do:

1. Find an area where you can safely create your pictures.
2. Plan out the overall design of the picture and let the children help you color in the larger areas. Or let the children design their own pictures, perhaps on a theme, such as different days of Creation or various Bible stories.
3. When you have finished the pictures, you might like to photograph them and then go somewhere to pray for the people who will see the artwork.

Another idea:

• On a beach you could draw patterns in the sand or create sand sculptures with biblical themes.

CHAPTER 2

City Parks

The Garden of Eden was a park planted and designed by God, and Adam and Eve spent their first Sabbath there.

Most cities have at least one park, and many have dozens of parks. The various parks in your city are worth exploring. Some cities publish an information guide to their parks and may also produce a calendar to show you when special events are taking place, such as free concerts, ecology and nature fairs, ranger-guided events, special walks, pond-dipping, and bird-watching. Some of these may make suitable and interesting Sabbath activities.

Each park is unique and will have its own special qualities. Exploring unfamiliar parks can become a special Sabbath adventure. You can find unusual plants, aviaries of birds, even free petting zoos. There may also be rivers, lakes, and woodlands to explore.

When in an unfamiliar park with children, you need to be especially streetwise for danger spots such as secluded areas where drug addicts or alcoholics may be gathering or discarding needles or broken containers. Make sure that your children are always within your sight.

You may be able to find information about your city's parks on your city's Web site.

Don't forget to take your Sabbath backpack with you!

• Pond-Dipping
• Tree-Visiting
• Playground Devotional
• Nature-Trail Scavenger Hunt
• Bible-Verse Scavenger Hunt
• Praise Balloons
• Creation Celebration
• Bible-Plant Hunt
• Bug Safari
• Bird Search

11

Pond-Dipping

Pond-dipping can be an interesting and absorbing activity for children. Often they are unaware of all the many things that live under the water that one must look carefully to see.

First of all, check whether your local parks are planning any pond-dipping activities in which you can participate. Or ask the parks department if certain ponds are especially good for dipping activities. You will also need to protect children from falling into the water.

THINGS YOU NEED:

- A book from the library about ponds and pond-dipping, or about the creatures that live in a pond, so that you can identify what you find
- Vinyl gloves to protect the skin from anything in the water that might be harmful
- Antibacterial hand cleanser for cleanup after this activity
- Small simple fishing nets
- Large white plastic container for collecting some pond water and looking at the creatures
- Magnifying glass to see some of the tiny creatures
- Small towel for drying arms, hands, and even feet!

What you do:

1. Dip the large white plastic container into the pond to collect some pond water.
2. Look at what you can find in the water you have collected. Use the nets to catch other things that may be in the pond, especially frog eggs, tadpoles, tiny fish, and other small life-forms.
3. Help your children identify what they have found and spend time looking carefully at how the creature moves. Encourage them to be gentle when handling the tiny creatures and to disturb them as little as possible.
4. Always return the creatures and their water to the pond when you have finished studying them.

Things to talk about:

- God's amazing creation and the detail that goes into little things that hardly anyone else can see.
- The way God has made us to depend on each other, just as the pond needs even the tiniest creatures in order to keep the pond community healthy and alive.
- How even small creatures can make a big difference.

12

Tree-Visiting

This is a simple activity that you can do in any park with trees, preferably where there are several similar trees close to each other.

THINGS YOU NEED:

- Blindfolds or scarves

What you do:

1. Blindfold a person and take them on a wiggly walk ending at a tree.
2. Guide their hands and body to explore the tree. Let them feel the bark, a leaf, the roots, the width of the tree, low branches, and anything else they can reach. Let them take a while to do this so that they can become closely acquainted with the tree.
3. Take them on a very wiggly walk away from the tree.
4. Remove the blindfold and discover whether they got to know their tree so well that they can find it again when they can see it!
5. Blindfold the other person and do the same thing all over again. It is quite amazing how soon you can get to know a tree!

Other ideas:

- Visit this tree at different times throughout the year to see how it changes.
- Take photographs of the tree throughout the year.
- Make a scrapbook about the tree, with pressed leaves and flowers, dried seeds, drawings of the tree during different seasons, bark rubbings made by placing paper on the bark and rubbing the side of an unwrapped crayon over the paper so that the pattern of the bark appears on the paper, and anything else unique to the tree.
- What creatures have you found in the tree? What can you find out about this kind of tree, and how is this tree especially useful for people?

Things to talk about:

- God's amazing creation of trees—why they are made the way they are, how their leaves and roots work, and how they grow and change through the seasons.
- Discuss how God has created our senses and how much we depend on our vision, but also how useful our sense of touch can be.
- Make a list of trees mentioned in the Bible. What trees are mentioned? Which Bible stories have special trees in them?
- Make a word-search puzzle of trees in the Bible or search for one on the Internet. Try <www.apuzzlezone.com/WordHunt/Trees_of_the_Bible.htm>.

13

Playground Devotional

Some parents may not be comfortable with their children playing on swings and slides and other playground equipment on Sabbath. Other parents let their children use this equipment because it can be a safe form of exercise that they may feel is needed after the child has sat in church for several hours.

Each parent and family needs to make this decision for themselves. Children who live in a city may not have the opportunity to burn off excess energy because they may not have their own yards to run in, trees to climb, or fields and safe pathways to walk along, and so a playground can offer some safe, contained space in which to exercise in a noncompetitive way.

One activity that can be done in a playground is to let the children use a piece of equipment, such as a swing, for a while and then to sit and talk about what swinging can teach us about Christian living and getting along together.

For example:
- Swinging can teach us that we also need to put some effort into our relationship with God and with each other. When we work at our relationship with God, just as when we work hard at swinging, we can go higher and see more and have more fun.
- We need to stay in contact with the swing to be safe and enjoy the ride.
- We need to look out for other people and make sure we don't hit them or knock them over. Sometimes we need to give each other some help and an encouraging little push to help them swing.
- Do any Bible texts come to mind when you think about these ideas?

You can do this activity for all kinds of equipment, such as slides, merry-go-rounds, seesaws, climbing apparatus, and anything else you find in the playground. It is amazing how many lessons you can learn about faith, Christian living, and caring for each other from a simple playground! Another benefit of this is that your child will often remember these ideas when he or she is playing on the swings and slides at other times. Perhaps you could take a photograph of each piece of equipment, write down all your ideas, and make a booklet about the lessons of God and life that you found in the playground.

14

Nature-Trail Scavenger Hunt

This is a scavenger hunt that you can use in a park. Give each child a small paper bag and a copy of the following list and let them see what they can find as they walk around the park with you. Make sure they are safe and go with them wherever possible. Check any regulations about what can be picked or removed from the park and be sure to obey the park's rules. You may want your child to wear protective rubber gloves for this activity. It is worth taking the time to debrief at the end of this activity and to let your child show you what he or she has collected and to talk about the objects that reminded them of God's love.

1. See if you can find the following things:
   A feather
   A piece of eggshell
   Something perfectly smooth
   Something that reminds you of an Old Testament story
   Something that reminds you of a parable
   Something that reminds you of God's love
   Something blue
   Three man-made objects that should have been taken home and thrown away
   A bone
   Something that would cling to your clothes
   Three different seeds
   Some animal hair or fluff or something soft
   A pretty stone
   Three different kinds of grass
2. See if you can fit them all in this bag!
3. Find someone to show all the things you have found and tell them why you have chosen them.
4. Take care of the environment.
5. Remember to wash your hands well afterward!

Bible-Verse Scavenger Hunt

This scavenger hunt for older children requires them to look up Bible verses and then to find the items in the verses.

THINGS YOU NEED:
- Bag
- Bible
- Pencil
- A copy of the following list of Bible references (without the answers)

What to do:
- Look for the items mentioned in each of the Bible verses below. This search has been based on the New International Version of the Bible. The answers have been included for you so that you can choose which items to include on your child's list, but give your child a list of only the Bible references.

Joshua 24:27	stone
Psalm 103:15	grass
Luke 8:11	seed
Isaiah 28:4	flower
Daniel 7:9	wool
Luke 15:8	coin
Luke 11:12	egg (eggshell)
Revelation 22:2	leaves
Isaiah 44:20	ashes (or something that has been burned)
Job 14:17	bag
1 Corinthians 3:12	wood (not the precious stones!)
2 Thessalonians 2:17	word (from some printed material)
2 Corinthians 12:7	thorn (but hopefully not in the flesh!)
Job 21:18	straw (of any kind)
Psalm 58:8	snail (just the shell)
Jeremiah 6:30	silver (or something that looks silvery)

Other ideas:
- Do this activity the other way round. Ask children to find twenty (or whatever number you choose) different objects that are mentioned in the Bible. When they have found them all, ask them to find a verse that mentions each item, using a Bible and concordance.
- Make a display of the objects and their verses, or create a shadow/memory box for them, pressing any leaves and flowers to help preserve them.

16

Praise Balloons

This can be a fun Sabbath activity for children of all ages.

THINGS YOU NEED:
- A do-it-yourself helium balloon kit (available from good greeting card stores and fancy goods stores). Choose one that has flat, unprinted, mylar balloons.
- Something to which the balloons can be secured so that they do not blow away and cause a litter hazard
- Permanent marker pens in a variety of colors (Protect your child's clothing from staining or wear old clothes, just in case the pens leave a mark.)
- Access to a picnic table or your own portable table as a firm base when decorating the balloons
- Scissors
- Ribbon or string

What you do:
1. Give each person a flat balloon to decorate with the marker pens. Encourage the children to write praise or witnessing slogans and to draw pictures or patterns on the balloons.
2. Have an adult carefully follow the instructions provided for inflating the balloons.
3. Tie the balloons to the children's hands or to a weighted handle, so that they don't blow away accidentally.
4. As you walk through the park, the balloons can be a witness or encouragement to passersby.

Other ideas:
- Invite other children in the park to decorate a balloon with an encouraging message and pictures, and let them take their balloons away with them.
- Decorate the balloons with feathers, ribbons, paper shapes, or other decorative items. Use adhesive tape to attach the items.

17

Creation Celebration

Sabbath is a celebration of creation, and this activity is a special celebration that you can do in a park. Invite some friends along to make the celebration extra special.

THINGS YOU NEED:

- Blindfold
- Jar of bubble soap
- Black paper
- Gummed stars
- Chenille stems (pipe cleaners)
- Glue
- Tissue
- Wiggle eyes
- Paper
- Crayons
- Special snacks

What you do:

Day one—light. Blindfold the child and guide her to touch various things in the park. See if she can guess what she is touching without seeing it. The blindfold makes everything dark. Then remove the blindfold and show her how beautiful everything is when it can be seen in the light.

Day two—atmosphere or air. Give the child a jar of bubble soap and a bubble wand and let him blow bubbles. Each bubble contains air and is like a tiny atmosphere of its own until it bursts. Talk about how God made the atmosphere like a big bubble around the earth and filled it with air so we could breathe (and blow bubbles).

Day three—water and land, flowers, trees, grass, fruits, and vegetables. If you are in a park, this should be easy! See if you can find water and land, trees, grass, flowers, etc. Take the time to look closely at some of the flowers in the park; even a daisy is very intricate and beautiful when you look at it closely. Perhaps you could photograph or draw the flowers.

Day four—sun, moon, and stars. Give your child a piece of black paper and some star stickers and let her make a picture of the night sky. If you have older children, encourage them to stick the stars in the pattern of actual constellations, referring to an astronomy book or Web sites to help them.

Day five—birds and fish. Give your child some colored chenille stems, glue, small wiggle eyes, tissue paper, etc., and let him create his own fish, bird, or insect.

Day six—animals. Play an animal guessing game. Family members can either act out different animals for others to guess or secretly choose an animal and invite others to ask them questions until someone guesses the answer.

Day six—human beings. God made us great! Have a time with your family when each person tells everyone else in the family something that you appreciate about him or her.

Day seven—God rested. Worship God for all the things He has created! Sing praise songs and pray thankful prayers. Celebrate with a picnic of simple foods, such as fruits and nuts, that would have been eaten in the Garden of Eden.

18

Bible-Plant Hunt

It can be surprising how many plants you can find in your local parks that are also mentioned in the Bible. How many can you find in each of your city's parks?

THINGS YOU NEED:

- Bible
- List of plants mentioned in the Bible, either from a Bible encyclopedia or from a Web site. Try <www.christiananswers.net/dictionary/plants.html>.
- Pencil
- Crayons
- Paper
- Camera
- Small concordance
- Pocket-sized tree-, plant- and flower-identification guides from a library

What you do:

1. Walk slowly around your local park, identifying the trees and plants and checking to see whether any of them are mentioned in the Bible.
2. You may like to photograph the plants you find and make a scrapbook or album of the Bible plants in your city's parks.
3. You can also make leaf and bark rubbings by laying paper on the underside of the leaves or over the bark and rubbing the side of an unwrapped crayon over the surface until the shape and pattern show through. These can be trimmed and added to your scrapbook. Seeds can be collected and dried and added to the scrapbook.
4. Do check any local laws about removing seeds and leaves from city parks.

Things to talk about:

Talk about how people in Bible times may have used the various plants. Use the Bible and your Bible encyclopedias to enrich your research.

Another idea:

- Follow this activity with a picnic of Bible foods!

Bug Safari

Wild animals may not be seen as often in the cities as they are in the countryside. But thousands of tiny creatures are still waiting to be discovered!

THINGS YOU NEED:

- Disposable gloves
- Notebook
- Magnifying glass
- Books for identifying insects
- Small penknife for peeling back bark from a dead tree
- Plastic box or glass jar for observing creatures
- Scissors
- Flashlight
- Pencil
- Camera
- String

What you do:
1. Before the activity, check whether any insects in your area are dangerous and know how to recognize them.
2. Find a place in the park that is natural and a bit wild.
3. You need to find some big flat stones that can be turned over or a piece of dead wood lying on the ground. Many creatures live and hide in these places, and it can be surprising how many species you can find under a stone or log. Watch the ground for ants and look for places where the ants may be nesting so you can watch them come and go.
4. Peel back some bark from a dead tree to see if there are any creatures under there too.
5. In a wooded area, make a small circle on the ground with the string. Look inside the circle and see how many creatures you can find under the leaves and on the ground. Take care not to be bitten by any of the creatures and be careful that they do not climb up your legs.
6. Watch the bugs and insects with your children. Notice how they move their legs and what happens when you touch them gently or shine a light on them. Look at what they seem to be eating and how they eat.
7. See if you can identify them using your reference books.

Other ideas:
- Make insects using ideas from children's craft books. Use paper, acetate, tissue, card, papier-mâché, egg cartons, paint, clothes pins, and chenille stems, or other craft supplies. You can find many insect craft projects by searching the Internet.
- Look up Bible verses about insects, such as ants and locusts. Use a Bible concordance to help you.

20

Bird Search

When we are in a city, we often don't notice how many tiny birds there are, and we don't hear their singing until we begin to search harder and listen more closely. How many can you find?

THINGS YOU NEED:
- A park to visit
- Something to sit or lie on
- A book of birds in your area

What you do:
1. Lie or sit very quietly and listen for the birds. Slowly you will begin to tune out all the city noises and hear some of the bird sounds. How many different ones can you hear? Can you tell which birds are making which sounds?
2. Sit still and look around for birds. Where can you see them? Can you identify them?
3. Come back a few weeks later and see if different birds are in your park.
4. Talk about birds in the Bible and God's care of all His creatures, even the tiniest little bird that falls softly to the ground.
5. Make a diary of the birds that you see and hear on different Sabbath bird searches.

Other ideas:
- Some parks have a bird blind in which you can sit and watch birds and match them to a chart on the wall. Often you can note on a blackboard when you have seen certain birds.
- If you don't have a park nearby, find a place to put up a bird-seed feeder or hummingbird feeder where you can see it from your window, or sit on a city bench and look for birds in your town square. It can even be interesting to watch pigeons!

CHAPTER 3

Animal Activities

God created an amazing array of plants and animals to delight us. Children particularly enjoy watching animals and learning about them because these creatures can be very entertaining and amusing.

Here are some animal activities that may enhance your Sabbaths.

- Adopt-a-Pet
- Special Animal Events at Zoos and Farms
- Animal Research
- Animal Scavenger Hunt
- Animal Treasure Hunt
- Bible Animals
- Close-Up Creatures
- Creature Camouflage
- Ark Interiors
- Design an Animal

21

Adopt-a-Pet

For many families in cities, pets are impractical or too expensive. Many city zoos or farms have schemes in which you can partially adopt an animal, learn more about it, and even have free tickets to visit the zoo or farm several times a year.

THINGS YOU NEED:
- Information on "adopting" an animal from the zoo or farm
- Money to finance the "adoption," which can be done prior to Sabbath

What you do:
1. Follow the procedure for adopting or sponsoring the animal.
2. Make the most of the adoption by learning all you can about the animal from the information the zoo or farm offers, researching about the animal, and visiting the animal frequently.
3. Make a diary of your visits to your adopted pet and take photographs, make drawings, and collect other information about the animal. Interview the animal's keeper and see if you can help feed or care for the animal in some way.

Other ideas:
- If you don't have the money or the opportunity to sponsor or adopt an animal, perhaps you could help take care of a pet in your neighborhood. Maybe you could take a dog for a walk on Sabbath and find out how to care for it.
- Perhaps there are other interesting pets you could visit in your locality.
- Maybe there are swans or geese in a local park that you could visit and feed. Make sure that you feed the birds appropriate grains because bread upsets the digestion of some birds. You may like to purchase special bird seeds and grain to take with you to feed the birds in your park. Which birds like eating the different grains?

22

Special Animal Events at Zoos and Farms

Often zoos and farms host special events where you can experience the animals in different ways.

THINGS YOU NEED:
- Information and events calendars from the zoos and farms in your area (Watch for events such as live nativities in winter, lambing in the spring, or special events focusing on a species of animals, or animals from a specific area of the world.)

What you do:
1. Explore the possibility of visiting any of these special events that might happen on Sabbath. Perhaps you could buy tickets in advance via the Internet or from the admissions office.
2. Make the most of these events by researching the animals before you go.

Another idea:
- Link your experiences at these events to stories in the Bible; for example, link lambing to Passover, the story of Abraham and Isaac and the sacrifice on the mountain, the story of the lost sheep, or the importance of sacrificial lambs in the Bible.

23

Animal Research

Often when we visit a zoo, we spend less than a minute looking at each animal! To appreciate God's amazing creation, maybe we need to spend more time understanding and learning about each creature! Just as God knows each one of us personally, He also knows each sparrow and every other animal He has created. By taking the time to research various animals, we increase our understanding and appreciation of God's amazing creation.

THINGS YOU NEED:
- Unless you have a free zoo in your city, an annual zoo pass is helpful, because then you don't feel you have to look at all of the animals in the zoo on one visit, and you can visit on Sabbath whenever you want.
- Several library books about the animal you want to research
- Information from Internet encyclopedias about the animal

What you do:
1. Go to the zoo and spend an hour watching one animal that interests your family or child. Perhaps you can arrange to interview the animal's keeper, too.
2. Give each person in your group a different book about the animal and invite them to discover something new and interesting about the animal being watched.
3. Invite older children to write a short report about the animal or at least a page of interesting things that they have learned.
4. This activity can be repeated for as many animals as you wish to study.

Other ideas:
- If there are no zoos in your area, perhaps you could visit a large pet store and watch the animals there. Sometimes these stores will let you handle the animals carefully, if a store assistant is with you.
- If you have access to the Internet, you can watch animals via webcams in their natural habitats at <www.africam.com>. This can be more interesting and exciting than going to your local zoo.
- If you have a drive-through safari park near you, it may be possible to pre-book tickets and drive through the park on Sabbath. Often you can drive through at your own pace and take time to watch the animals. Do follow all the safety precautions.

24

Animal Scavenger Hunt

This is a fun activity to do in a zoo, especially with younger children.

THINGS YOU NEED:
- A written "scavenger" list of animal features that might be found in the zoo, such as
  - an animal that eats bananas
  - a bird that has green feathers
  - an animal that lives in a tree
  - a creature that eats fish
  - an animal that is smaller than you
  - an animal that is mentioned in the Bible
  - a creature that has no legs
  - an animal (not a bird) that has some blue coloring
  - an animal that you were able to touch
  - an animal that comes from Australia
  - an animal that you saw hugging its baby
  - the funniest animal you saw
- Pencils
- Clipboards

What you do:
1. Go around the zoo with your child, looking for the various animals that fit these descriptions.
2. Let your child write the names of the animals on the scavenger sheet as you find them.

Other ideas:
- Photograph the animals that fit the scavenger list descriptions.
- Create a photo scavenger hunt for prereading children, using pictures from a simple computer graphic program, the Internet, or your own drawings of animals.
- Ask the zoo if they have their own worksheets for children to use. Sometimes they offer a small prize for children who complete a worksheet. If they charge money for the sheet, you might be able to arrange to buy it in advance.

25

Animal Treasure Hunt

This is different from the scavenger hunt and is suitable for older children.

THINGS YOU NEED:

- Bibles
- Pencils
- Paper

What you do:

1. Write the letters of a Bible name vertically down the left side of your piece of paper, with one letter per line.
2. Find an animal in the zoo that begins with each letter in the Bible name, and write their names next to the letters you wrote first. It may be helpful to visit the zoo first, without your children, so that you can find out which animals are in the zoo's collection and some of the information posted about each animal. This can help you to create and check the treasure hunt on your own before Sabbath.
3. Create some clues for the animal using information posted about them or visual clues, such as their color and shape or special features.

Here is an example for younger children. Older children could have more complex clues:

1. M—meerkat	These little creatures live in the ground but they like popping up and looking around!
2. O—orangutan	This creature is orange, but not quite a fruit! He wears a very hairy suit!
3. R—rabbit	This animal hops with a white fluffy tail And he moves very fast, so he's not like a snail!
4. D—deer	This animal has a mom called a doe And dad has antlers to fight off the foe.
5. E—elephant	This creature is huge when he stands and he has a long nose that he uses like hands!
6. C—camel	This animal is known as a desert ship; You could have a ride, but take care not to slip!
7. A—alligator	This animal has a toothy long smile And lives in the rivers, just like the Nile!
8. I—iguana	This is a reptile with wiggly eyes Don't try to copy him; you'll have a surprise!

When you give the clues to your child, include numbered clues and spaces for them to write their answers. As they find the answers to the clues, they will uncover the name of the Bible character or the letters to create a Bible verse.

26

Bible Animals

Watching some of the various animals mentioned in the Bible can help us to have a deeper understanding of some of the Bible stories.

THINGS YOU NEED:

- Bibles
- Bible concordance
- Pencils
- Paper
- Clipboards

What you do:

1. Visit a farm or zoo and specifically focus on the animals that are mentioned in the Bible. Goats, sheep, and camels may be obvious, but many other animals are mentioned in the Bible. If you visit <www.christiananswers.net/dictionary/animals.html>, you will find more than 120 animals mentioned, such as badger, mole, viper, vulture, and peacock.
2. Hunt for any animals mentioned in the Bible and spend time watching them and reading the Bible verses that mention the animals.
3. Talk together about how observing these animals helped you deepen your understanding of the Bible passages.

Other ideas:

- If a zoo or farm is not accessible to you, hunt for animals in your neighborhood and observe them. Most people can find some ants, bees, worms, caterpillars, sparrows, or doves nearby.
- Instead of going outside, use books and the Internet to study the animals. You may be able to find video clips of some creatures on the Internet.
- Borrow videos or DVDs about animals and creation, or record nature programs from your television. Try finding videos in the series called Incredible Creatures That Defy Evolution from <www.explorationfilms.com>.

27

Close-Up Creatures

Some creatures can be kept for a short time at home and watched closely, providing an excellent learning experience for children, without the long-term commitment needed by a larger pet.

THINGS YOU NEED:

- A simple ant, worm, or caterpillar kit. These may be available from good educational toy suppliers or by mail order. Ants and worms may be easy to find, but caterpillar kits usually come with a voucher so you can order the caterpillars when you choose and then watch them go through their stages until they become butterflies, which you can release in a park.

What you do:

1. Follow the instructions for your kit very carefully. Involve your child in setting up the kit and finding the creatures for your kit.
2. Take the time on Sabbath to observe the creatures closely and watch how they move and eat and respond to their environment. You could even write a diary about how the caterpillar changes and what happens each day. You could combine the caterpillar diary with crafts to make a caterpillar, chrysalis, and butterfly.
3. Make a caterpillar from lots of colored paper circles, stuck in a wiggly row on a piece of paper. Or make one out of a long section of an egg carton and give it chenille legs.
4. Make a chrysalis from crumpled paper, scrunching it into a chrysalis shape and sticking it to a branch so that it hangs down like a chrysalis.
5. Make a butterfly by folding a piece of paper in half and opening it out. Then add daubs of paint to one side of the paper and fold the paper over, pressing firmly, to create a symmetrical pattern. Cut a butterfly shape out of this paper, and add a black strip of paper for a body and two black chenille antennae.

Another idea:

- Visit a butterfly farm nearby where you could have a prepaid visit. How many butterflies can you find there? Can you watch the eggs hatching, the caterpillars creeping, and the chrysalises hanging?

28

Creature Camouflage

Understanding how God's design of camouflage protects animals can help us to appreciate the care He takes to protect us.

THINGS YOU NEED:
- Bibles
- Bible concordance
- Books or pictures of animals using camouflage for their protection
- Household items that can be "hidden" using camouflage in your yard or living room

What you do:
1. Read in the Bible about God's protection of you and your family. Use a concordance to help you find passages, such as Psalm 18, or stories of God's protection, such as the stories of Joseph, Jonah, Daniel, and Esther.
2. Talk about how God created the animals in special ways to offer them protection. Show how moths can be hidden against the bark of a tree, frogs can hide in greenish-brown swamps, chameleons change their color, chrysalises look like dried leaves, and stick-insects look like the bushes on which they feed. Research into some of the different types of camouflage there are at <www.science.howstuffworks.com/animal-camouflage.htm>.
3. Hide an assortment of objects in your living room or yard so that they are camouflaged.
4. Invite your child to look for the items and to think about how each item was camouflaged. For example, hang a wire whisk in a tree, or plant it in the garden and it might look like a plant or twigs. Lay a small piece of cloth on your floor that matches the color of your carpet. Place an egg close to a pile of stones, and a piece of crumpled white tissue in a flower bed where there are other white flowers.
5. When your child has found the hidden objects, give him or her the opportunity to hide some other items in places where they will be camouflaged for you to find.
6. Thank God for His generous protection of His creatures and tell stories of the ways in which He has protected you in the past.

Another idea:
- Let your child think of other ways in which God has designed animals for their protection, such as putting quills on a porcupine.

29

Ark Interiors

When we read the story of Noah's ark, we could be very curious about what the ark looked like inside and how all the animals were kept comfortable and safe!

THINGS YOU NEED:

- Bibles
- A trip to the zoo
- Pencils
- Paper
- Clipboards
- Crayons
- Scissors
- Large sheet of paper
- Paper glue

What you do:

1. Read the story of Noah's ark in Genesis 6:1 to Genesis 9:17.
2. Think about how the animals fit into the ark. How would you have designed the ark so that they would all have fit inside? What did the different animals need? How would they be fed and cleaned?
3. Give each person several animals to consider that live in the zoo you are visiting.
4. Give each person a pencil, paper, and clipboard and invite them to design a place for their animal to live in the ark.
5. Later share your designs with each other. Perhaps you could cut out the different dens and work out how they might have been placed in the ark. Add other animal dens to the design. Remember to design a good place for the humans to live too!

Another idea:

- Create 3-D dens for animals in the ark out of different sized boxes and house your child's toy animal collection in them.

30

Design an Animal

This is another animal-themed activity that can be done at home.

THINGS YOU NEED:

- Pencils
- Paper
- All kinds of craft materials
- String
- Adhesive
- Fabric
- Scissors

What you do:
1. Create instructions for your child or family to design an animal. For example, the instructions might be to design an animal that could live happily on the top of your apartment block or in the yard at school or that would be an ideal pet to suit your family. Make the instructions as detailed as you like and be very creative about where the animal might have to live.
2. Invite your family or child to think about how to design the animal. What would it need to eat? How would it eat? How would it move around? What shape and color would it be, and why? What special habits might it have?
3. Once you have thought about the animal and collected lots of ideas, try making a model of the animal out of the materials you have collected.
4. As you do this, talk about how God might have designed the animals. How are God's designs different from ours? How might God have designed the animal you are trying to make?
5. Encourage an appreciation of the challenge of creation and the wisdom of God to create creatures perfectly suited to their different habitats. He has also created each one of us with careful thought to suit the environments in which He has placed us.

Other ideas:
- Draw the animal instead of trying to make it with craft materials, name the creature, and write a description of it for an imaginary encyclopedia.
- Work as a group on one animal, or let older children make their own animals and then talk about their designs at the end of the activity. You could each have the same instructions and see how the designs vary, or you could have different instructions.

CHAPTER 4

Visiting Museums and Places of Interest on Sabbath

Museums may seem to be unusual places to visit on Sabbath, but they can contain a rich resource for families wanting to explore different aspects of God's character together.

Many museums are free or let you buy tickets in advance, either at the ticket booth or on the Internet. If you have a museum that is especially good to visit on Sabbath, you could consider purchasing season tickets for your family. Other museums may have free entry if you visit later in the day, which could suit a Sabbath-afternoon activity.

It is worth visiting the museum beforehand so that your family's Sabbath visit can be well planned and focused. Some museums provide their own trails and activities for families and children, and you may like to preview these before you go, in case they will be useful for Sabbath activities. It can also be useful to purchase a guidebook for the museum before your Sabbath visit, so you can read about special things to look out for.

Take drinks and snacks with you so that you don't have to pay to use the museum cafeteria. If it could be hard to steer your child past the museum gift store, you may like to buy a tiny treat for them from the store during the week and let them have the gift when it is time to leave the museum.

This section offers a range of activity ideas that you may like to use if you have access to museums and galleries in your town and you feel comfortable visiting them on Sabbath.

- Art Galleries
- Natural History Museums—Plants and Animals
- Natural History Museums/Science Museums—Human Body
- Libraries
- Ethnic Museums
- Archaeological Museums
- Geological Museums
- Churches
- Planetariums
- Religious Communities

31

Art Galleries

Some art galleries contain paintings of various Bible stories. Go on a hunt together to see how many paintings you can find that show a scene from a Bible story.

THINGS YOU NEED:

- Sketch pad
- Pen
- Crayons

What to do:

1. If you have a guidebook and know where you will find the paintings, take the children straight to the pictures and see if the children can guess the Bible story that inspired the artist.
2. Take coloring materials and let the children make their own copies of the paintings, to create their own Bible art gallery or scrapbook.
3. Discuss questions such as these:
   - If the Bible story were placed in a contemporary setting, how might the artist have painted the picture?
   - Why did the artist choose to spend so much time and effort creating this picture from the Bible?
   - What do you think the artist was trying to tell us about the people in the painting, or about God, when he or she painted the picture?
   - Ask how the picture is different from the ideas the children have about the Bible story, or whether it is similar to their ideas about the Bible story, and let this open up a discussion about the different characters and actions in the story.
4. Children who like to write might like to rewrite the Bible story in their own words, using the painting to add to their understanding of the story, or to write the Bible story from the perspective of one of the people in the painting.
5. Play "I spy" with the painting to challenge family members to look for details in the painting beginning with a specific letter of the alphabet. What unusual things can you find in the pictures?
6. Perhaps your family could create its own gallery trail and make a simple workbook for other families to use when visiting the museum on Sabbath. This can contain questions about the paintings, unusual features that you noticed, and questions about the Bible stories that are depicted in the paintings. These could then be shared with other families in your city who may like to visit the art gallery.
7. Even if you don't have an art gallery in your town or city, you can visit some excellent art galleries online and take virtual tours through them to see the paintings.

32

Natural History Museums— Plants and Animals

Natural history museums are great places to visit on Sabbath because they contain so much information about some of the wonderful things God made, how our bodies work, and all about plants and animals.

Even though these museums often include information based on evolutionary theories and time spans, there is usually much more information about the amazing way in which creatures and plants have been designed.

THINGS YOU NEED:

- Paper or notebook
- Pen or pencil

What to do:
1. If your children are involved in Adventurer or Pathfinder programs, it may be worth finding out the requirements for some of the nature honors, because these can help to focus your time in the museum, and the children can also earn their awards.
2. Ask the museum information desk for any children's worksheets that may be available. If they charge for the worksheets, find a way to purchase them in advance. If they don't produce worksheets for the general public, ask if you can have the education information pack that they make available to teachers planning school visits to the museum.
3. Rather than being tempted to rush around the museum and see everything quickly, focus on one section at a time, so that your child can learn as much as they are able to absorb.
4. A useful question that can lead to an interesting family discussion is What does the way this creature or plant was designed tell you about God?
5. Write the letters of the alphabet down the left side of a piece of paper and hunt throughout the natural history museum for animals or plants that begin with the different letters of the alphabet.
6. Look in the "Animal Activities" section of this book for other ideas that could be adapted to a natural history museum.

33

Natural History Museums/ Science Museums—Human Body

Some natural history or science museums have special sections that explore the wonders of the human body and how it works. These often have excellent interactive activities and computer programs to help us understand more about how our bodies work, the benefits of healthful living, the dangers of tobacco and alcohol use, etc.

What to do:
1. If you can visit an exhibition like this, it is an amazing opportunity to help your children to understand the wonder of their own body and how they have been created by God for His glory.
2. If you can't visit an exhibition, create your own activities using educational material for children designed to help them learn about the human body.

Internet search terms:
   human body, education, children

34

Libraries

Libraries can be a resource for Sabbaths because you can borrow resources to use at home on Sabbath, or you can visit the library on Sabbath as part of a special project. Do check opening times before you go and whether the library is having any special activity sessions that could be distracting for your family. Sometimes the special library activities may work well as Sabbath activities. If you are not sure, ask the librarians involved about their plans. See whether you can be added to their mailing list so that you can make use of any appropriate sessions that they might offer.

Being intentional about visiting a library can help children focus on the books and the projects that you are working on together because there can be fewer distractions than at home, and there can be a novelty about the library setting that can make the experience special. Libraries are also peaceful places, with comfortable chairs and workspaces that can help families maintain a spiritual atmosphere.

What to do:
1. Find special Bible story books to read in the library or at home. Let your child help choose the stories he wants you to read to him or the ones he wants to read on his own.
2. Use the library to help you find resources that will help your child do a special project on the countries where your church is supporting mission projects. How do the people live in those countries? What would it be like to be a child in the country? What do people in the country eat? What are their houses like? What are the special needs of that country?
3. Research life during Bible times. Find books in the history and religion sections that will help your children find out what it would have been like to have been a child in Jesus' time, or what life may have been like in Egypt or Canaan during Bible times.
4. Download Adventurer or Pathfinder honor requirements on nature topics, and use the library to help your children research the answers and make scrapbooks or project files to complete the nature honors. The focus of this activity is to help children appreciate the wonder of God's amazing creation.
5. Many libraries offer free Internet access. If you don't have Internet access at home, you may like to explore some interesting Christian Web sites or nature and educational sites that have material that you consider appropriate for Sabbath. Search the Internet for Bible activities for children and other sites mentioned in this book.

35

Ethnic Museums

Some cities have special ethnic, cultural, or anthropological museums. These may offer great opportunities for children to learn about other cultures and countries. The more children learn about other cultures, the more likely they are to appreciate and understand people who are different from them.

You could arrange to visit a museum or center representing the area where you know missionaries or where you are supporting mission work with your gifts.

What to do:
1. Find out if there are special events at the ethnic museum, such as musical events during which visitors are shown how to play traditional musical instruments or events at which you can taste traditional foods.
2. Help your child understand how other people live, what their homes, clothes, and food are like, what they do for work and fun, and how their beliefs differ from your beliefs.
3. You could plan to return home for a special supper of foods from the country you have learned about in the museum.
4. Perhaps you could arrange an international event at your church, to which people bring their traditional foods for others to taste and give a short presentation about their own cultures.

36

Archaeological Museums

Some archaeological museums have items that have been uncovered from the Middle Eastern Bible lands, and these can be very interesting to visit because they can help us understand more about Bible times and how people lived, worked, and worshiped together. Other museums may have Roman artifacts that would also have been widely used during the time of Jesus.

You will need to know what is in the museum that you plan to visit so that you can decide how it will best fit with your plans for Sabbath activities.

- Some museums can be very interesting and interactive, and you can try on clothes like those worn in ancient times or make your own oil-lamp out of clay, like those used in Bible times.
- If there are no museums like these in your area, try searching the Internet for Bible time crafts, archaeology of Bible lands, etc., or visit <www.bibarch.com>.

37

Geological Museums

Some towns have geological museums where you can study rocks and various gem stones as well as how mountains and valleys are made and how the landscape has been carved.

If you have such a museum in your area, it could be an interesting place to visit on Sabbath. Often these museums have timescales that do not correspond to our understanding of Creation, but there are also many things that can be learned and experienced in a geological museum.

What to do:

1. Go to the museum and read Revelation 21:10–27 together. This passage describes the amazing Holy City of Jerusalem, with its foundations of precious stones. As you go around the museum, look for the stones mentioned in the Bible. You may need to use a modern translation so that the names used for the stones in the Bible are the same names that would be used today in the museum. You could let your child draw a picture of the Holy City and color the foundations to match the different stones mentioned there. Imagine together how glorious the city will look.

2. As you look at the stones, marvel at God's amazing creativity in designing such beautiful stones that are often hidden in the earth where we can't see them.

3. As you think about the stones that you see in the museum, look for insights into God's character and object lessons or parables that may come to your mind. For example, there are geodes that look like ordinary stones on the outside, but when they are cracked open they reveal beautiful colored crystals inside. Or consider the diamonds that are formed from dense black carbon that has been placed under enormous pressure.

4. Talk about various Bible stories that mention stones.

5. If you cannot visit a geological museum, you could visit a local rock and gem store and look at the different colored stones there. Or you could use a library book or search the Internet for geological sites, such as <www.geology.wisc.edu/~museum>, which offers a virtual tour and other activities.

38

Churches

Some cities have churches that are open during the day. Churches of various denominations have different kinds of buildings and worship experiences.

What to do:

1. Churches of special interest often have activity sheets for children to complete as they look around the church, with stories about different things in the church and unusual objects to look for or words to find. If a church you want to visit doesn't have a children's activity sheet, perhaps you could create your own.

2. One simple way of creating an activity is to use a digital camera to photograph items of special interest in the church. Print these on one sheet of paper and see if your child can find them as you explore the building together.

3. Perhaps the churches in your area could have an open day where you can visit each other's churches, learn about each church's history, and search for the unique aspects of each building.

Questions to ask:

- What do the things in this church tell you about God, and what do they say to you?
- How is this church different from other churches that you have seen?
- What do you like most about this church?
- What ideas from this church would you like to see in your church?

4. You might like to consider visiting a synagogue on Sabbath. Ask first to check that you would be allowed to visit and whether there is anything you might need to know about how to behave, where to sit, or what to do. It can be very interesting to see how another religion celebrates Sabbath. What can you learn from this experience that you would like to incorporate into your own family's experience of Sabbath? Perhaps you could also spend Friday evening with a Jewish family as they welcome the Sabbath in their own unique way.

39

Planetariums

If you are fortunate enough to have a good planetarium in your town, it can be lovely to lie back and watch the stars and explore space in comfort and safety! Again, you would need to prebook and pay for your seats before Sabbath.

What to do:
1. While the planetarium show is running, it is wonderful to think about the greatness of a God who created the entire universe and far more stars and planets than we can see!
2. You can imagine traveling through space when we are in heaven and visiting other planets that no one on earth has ever seen yet!
3. It is interesting to learn about the constellations during the show so that you can identify them at night when you have the opportunity to lie under a clear starry sky.
4. Think about the stories in the Bible in which the sun, moon, or stars were significant, such as guiding the wise men to Jesus.
5. If you cannot visit a planetarium, try visiting <www.fourmilab.ch/yoursky/> or other Web sites where you can explore the sky. Or search the Internet for "virtual telescope" sites.
6. You may also find that there is an observatory near you where you can go and watch the sky through special telescopes.
7. Find out the times when you are likely to see shooting stars in your skies. Spend a Friday evening in a dark area, where there are no street or town lights, and lie on a blanket, looking for constellations and shooting stars. Take a thermos of a hot beverage to help keep you warm.

40

Religious Communities

In some places there are Christian communities who live and work together according to special religious guidelines. It can be very interesting to take the time to visit one of these. Find out if the community is open to visitors and when you can visit. Ask if there are special guidelines that you need to know about, such as a dress code, or any other ways in which you can show respect to the community and not cause offense during your visit.

Many communities welcome visitors and are happy to talk about their way of life and what inspires them. Often there are good principles of sharing, supporting each other, spending time with God, serving others, not being materialistic, and caring for the environment. What can you learn as you visit this community that will inspire you as a family and help you to live more closely to God and to each other?

Some communities that may be open to visitors:

Hutterite, Mennonite, certain monasteries and convents, retreat centers, Christian art- or music-based communities, specific ministry-focused communities (such as those ministering to refugees, or people with HIV/AIDS).

CHAPTER 5

Ideas for Sharing God's Love With Others

In Matthew 12:12, Jesus talked about the importance of doing good on the Sabbath day. Jesus healed people on the Sabbath day to emphasize the importance of caring for others on the Sabbath.

Here are some projects that you might be able to do in your community to share the love of Jesus with others.

- Community Clean-Up
- Visiting Retirement Homes
- Caring for the Homeless
- Give or Take
- Give-Aways
- Practical Service Ideas
- Shoe-Box Gifts
- Adopt-a-Grandparent
- Adopt-a-Missionary
- Volunteer Projects

41

Community Clean-Up

There are many spoiled places in cities, where the beauty of creation has been obscured by garbage, graffiti, and deterioration.

When one church in London, England, asked the people in their community what they would most like their church to do, the people said, "Please help clean up our community!" The church was surprised by this request, but they created a slogan, designed a T-shirt and posters, and went to work, cleaning up the vacant lots and the debris around the streets. They also worked together with the local city sanitation department to find the safest and best way of cleaning up graffiti and garbage, and they were provided with protective clothing, bags, and pick-up sticks.

THINGS YOU NEED:

- Permission (perhaps) for your clean-up project from your local city sanitation department. It is only polite to inform them, and they may be willing to provide you with useful information, equipment, and support.
- Protective clothing and tools for picking up garbage safely
- Garbage bags
- A collection point for all the garbage so that it can easily be removed once it has been collected

What you do:
1. Collect garbage and clean up the area that you have chosen.
2. Remove the garbage from the area or arrange for it to be collected by the city sanitation team.
3. Mow grass, pull weeds, and make the area look more attractive.

Other ideas:
- If all these ideas seem too big for you or too difficult to sustain in your neighborhood, perhaps you could plant some pots with a selection of colorful flowers and give them to people who need some encouragement or something beautiful to remind them of God's creative love.
- Sponsor a vacant lot and keep it clean and tidy, or participate in an adopt-a-road program.

42

Visiting Retirement Homes

Many senior citizens in retirement homes would enjoy regular visits from a family or church group. It is probably better to visit one place regularly and to build up friendships with the residents than to visit many different places.

THINGS YOU NEED:
- A friendly retirement home where you and your family would be welcome to visit

What you do:
1. Talk to the manager of the home to find out if there are any particular wishes he or she might have for your visit.
2. You could make and take treats to the residents throughout the year, according to the seasons. If you take food items, be aware that some of the residents may have special diets. Floral arrangements, cards, bookmarks, and tiny gifts can be simple and inexpensive, and take up little space in their small rooms.
3. If you are musical, perhaps you could organize a short musical program to perform in the home.
4. Many older people like to be able to tell younger people the stories of their lives. Perhaps your child could create a project by collecting the stories the older people have to tell about a certain time in their history or their families or the wisdom they have collected that they would like to pass on to the next generation. Their stories could be recorded and collected to inspire your child and future generations.

Another idea:
- Instead of a retirement home, choose a center for people with disabilities.

43

Caring for the Homeless

Many churches in cities support programs that care for the homeless people in their communities. Helping with these programs can be a constructive and caring way to spend Sabbaths together as a family, because children are often inspired by serving those who are especially needy.

THINGS YOU NEED:

- To make contact with a homeless charity in your area and to find out how you can help them

What you do:

1. Provide the kind of help needed by the charity that you can offer as a family, or join up with other families in your church if the project is too big for your own family.

2. Young children can help prepare the vegetables for making soup, because this can be made at home or in a church hall. Children can also pour beverages, make sandwiches, and put together small bags of healthful snacks to take away. They could pack bags of simple toiletry supplies, such as tissues, wipes, soap, deodorant, combs, shampoo, toothbrushes, and toothpaste. These can all be done by children without the danger of them having to meet with the homeless people, if this might place them at risk. However, if it is safe and possible, it can be a good idea for children to see how extreme poverty, homelessness, and drug and alcohol use can affect people's lives.

Other ideas:

- Centers for refugees and homeless people often need adults who can offer services such as hair-cutting, medical attention, legal and financial advice, and dental care.
- Clean secondhand clothing and supplies of new underwear are often needed by this community. Warm clothes and blankets are needed in winter, and older children may be able to cut colorful fleece fabrics into cozy scarves to give away.

44

Give or Take

One unusual service project is to run a "Give or Take" project. This can be an interesting way to get to know some of the people in your community.

THINGS YOU NEED:

- Large basket
- Sturdy cart
- A few cans of food
- Small printed flyers about your project (optional)

What you do:

1. Knock on someone's door, smile, introduce yourself, and explain that you are Christians and you are involved in a caring project for your community. Explain that you are collecting cans of food for a specific project, but that you are aware that many people in your community may need food too.
2. Invite them to "give a can or take a can." They can either donate a can of food from their cupboards to the project, or they can take a can from your basket for their own use.
3. You may like to let people know that any extra cans collected at the end of the day will be donated to a well-known local charity, such as a women's shelter, a refugee center, or homeless project.
4. Adapt how you introduce this project to people depending on the needs and culture of your community.

Another idea:

- Take a choir or ensemble to a public place to sing. Instead of collecting for a charity, give out small gifts such as bookmarks, apples, or wrapped candy. It surprises people to be given something rather than being asked for a contribution!

45

Give-Aways

It can be interesting to see what happens when you try to give something away!

THINGS YOU NEED:

- Something to give away that will be appreciated
- Perhaps some computer-printed labels with an encouraging message that lets people know that you are giving these items away because you want to share Jesus' love with them

Suggestions of things to give away:
Small bottles of water on a hot day
Ice-cream bars in a park close to a children's playground
Pens or pencils with Bible promises printed on them
Individual flowers to women on Mothers' Day weekend
Healthful commercially packaged snack bars
Bottles of bubble soap for small children
Free face-painting for children in a park
Small candles with a message of peace close to Christmas

What you do:
1. Decide what you will give and where you will give it away.
2. Purchase or make the items and any labels or tags that will let people know that you are giving these things away because you want to share God's love.
3. Set up a place where you can give things away. You may need a small table and a cooler. You may also need a place to keep extra supplies.
4. Let children and adults go together to give the items. Adults will often take things from a child that they may not take from another adult. It is also important to keep the child safe from strangers.

Another idea:
- When you have given everything away, sit down and talk about your experiences. You may need to talk to your children about why some people are reluctant to receive gifts from people they don't know.

46

Practical Service Ideas

One special gift you can give to people in your church and community is practical service. Some of these ideas might seem unusual to do on Sabbath because they might be considered "work." It is important that both you and the person you are serving are comfortable with whatever you are doing for them if you are doing this on Sabbath. Sadly, we are often too busy during the week to do these acts of service on other days, and, if so, we may seriously need to address our own time schedules and priorities.

We may not be able to heal a man's withered hand as Jesus did, but there may be small acts of service that we can offer others that could make a significant difference in their life while also speaking volumes about God's love. Sabbath is sacred and precious and not a day for us to do work for our own benefit. However, we may need to ask ourselves some challenging questions about the purpose of Sabbath if we are so concerned to keep our Sabbath perfectly that we are reluctant to relieve the burdens of those around us. Some people have found themselves to be especially blessed by performing an act of generous service on Sabbath for someone who really needed it.

Some ideas for you to consider:
1. Offer Sabbath lunch to a family who would not be able to return the favor. If they have children, ask them what they would most like to eat and then make that for lunch.
2. Take care of a family of children for a Sabbath afternoon so that their parents can have a rest or spend time together. Or do this for a single parent who is exhausted from trying to study as well as work to care for her family.
3. Clean the kitchen of a person who is disabled or a single parent.
4. Weed the garden of an elderly person whose garden has become too much for him or her to manage.
5. Decorate the room of a shut-in, so that he or she has clean and cheerful surroundings.
6. Bake cookies or home-made bread to take to a refugee family or a new family in your community.

47

Shoe-Box Gifts

Creating gift shoe boxes for children overseas can be a fun and rewarding service project for young children.

THINGS YOU NEED:

- Instructions and guidelines from the organization collecting the shoe boxes
- Sturdy shoe boxes with lids
- A selection of prepurchased items to go in the shoe boxes (If possible, let your child help you choose some of the items to go in the box.)
- Gift wrap
- Tape
- Scissors

What you do:

1. Cut the gift wrap into pieces of appropriate sizes for the objects to be packed, and let your child help you wrap the various items. Show her what to do and help her, so that she learns how to wrap gifts neatly.
2. Let your child pack the objects in the box and, as you do so, imagine together how the child who receives the box will enjoy all the gifts you have included.
3. When the box has been packed, have a special prayer to bless the box and the child who will receive it.
4. Let your child take the box to the collection depot.

Other ideas:

- If possible, from the agency collecting the gifts, borrow a video about their work or about the children who will receive the boxes.
- Involve your child in other gift projects in your own community, such as projects that provide gifts for children who have a parent in prison. Some cities also run wish lists to provide children from low-income families with special birthday gifts.

48

Adopt-a-Grandparent

Perhaps your child's grandparents live a long way from you. Perhaps there are seniors in your church whose grandchildren live a long way from them. Perhaps you could adopt a grandparent to share some happiness.

THINGS YOU NEED:
- A senior willing to be "adopted" as a grandparent

What you do:
1. Accompany your child on short visits to the adopted grandparent. You might like to help your child choose a simple gift to take, such as a flower, a card he has made, a small cake he helped you bake, or decorated cookies.
2. Help your child build a relationship with the adopted grandparent by asking questions about what the senior person likes to do, what his hobbies are, special stories about his life, adventures he had, how he came to be a Christian, and some of the special things God has done for him over the years.
3. Perhaps the grandparent could teach your child a special skill or take an interest in your child's hobbies. Perhaps he could come to supper at your home or accompany your family on a Sabbath outing or picnic.

Another idea:
- Adopt aunts and uncles and cousins or whatever other family members you would like to adopt into your own family!

49

Adopt-a-Missionary

Many missionaries and their families appreciate some personal encouragement, prayers, and practical support from people in their home country.

THINGS YOU NEED:

- Contact information of a missionary who would appreciate your support (Perhaps you can get to know a missionary family who are about to leave for mission service or a missionary family who are home on furlough, so that you make personal contact with them before they leave.)

What you do:

1. Contact the missionary by email or letter, letting them know that your family wishes to support them.
2. Find out what their prayer requests are, so that you can pray for their specific needs.
3. Are there any ways you could support them practically? Some missionaries need Christian magazines, lesson quarterlies, children's Sabbath School supplies, art and craft materials, or other supplies specific to the needs of their community. Could you collect these things from your church members to send to the missionary?
4. On certain Sabbaths you could focus on your missionary family, writing letters of encouragement, creating care packages, packing supplies to send, and praying for the family in a specific way. You could read their letters or emails, learn more about the community where they are serving, and serve foods that would be eaten in the country or research current news of the country so that you are informed about the issues that could be affecting their ministry and the needs of the community around them.

Other ideas:

- Adopt a student missionary and encourage them in different ways throughout their time overseas.
- Perhaps young people you know from your own community are serving overseas and would appreciate care packages from home.

50

Volunteer Projects

Often volunteer offices have long lists of volunteer projects that need occasional or regular commitment. There could be dogs that need walking, pathways to check in nature reserves, signs to check as you walk around national parks, people who need befriending, garbage to clear, and even birds to identify and count for nature surveys.

THINGS YOU NEED:
- To make contact with your local volunteer office and ask for a list of volunteer opportunities within your community

What you do:
1. Prayerfully read the list of volunteer opportunities within your community. You will need to think about how much time will be appropriate for you to spend volunteering on Sabbaths with your family. You will also need to appreciate the needs of your own family and children when you consider which volunteer projects might work for you.
2. Volunteer only for tasks that you can manage easily, so that you don't let people down. Choose projects that fit comfortably within your concept of appropriate Sabbath activities and suit your own spiritual gifts and talents.
3. Whatever you choose to do, you will be a witness to the community and project for which you are volunteering, and your child will learn how much fun it can be to help other people and projects.

Another idea:
- If there is nothing on the volunteer list that suits your family, you might like to offer your own special gifts as a service to the volunteer project. One family decided to offer weekend relief care for a disabled child. One weekend a month the child would stay with the Christian family, go to church with them, and experience Sabbath in their home, to give her parents a break. The children learned how to relate to a child with a disability and enjoyed finding new ways to play with the child and entertain her.

Indoor Activities

CHAPTER 6

Almost-Instant Bible Games

Everyone has Sabbaths when they are very tired, the weather changes and they have to stay inside, or someone is sick and the family needs to stay home to care for them.

Here are some games to play that don't need very much preparation or special equipment.

- Bible-Story Scavenger Hunt
- Bible-Name Acrostic Stories
- Bible-Promise Search
- Bible Video-Clip Quiz
- Bible-Verse Race
- Rainbow "Thank You" Search
- Bible-Name Chain
- Bible-Categories Quiz
- Bible-Object Creations
- Proverbial Presentations

51

Bible-Story Scavenger Hunt

THINGS YOU NEED:

- Bibles
- Small container, such as a paper bag, basket, or bowl for each person

What you do:

1. Give each person a small container and a Bible.
2. Invite them to choose a story from the Bible and to read it carefully and silently, so that nobody else knows which story they have chosen.
3. Then each person needs to go on a scavenger hunt through the home to find three things that are mentioned in the story, or their modern day equivalents. (For example, if the story mentions a lamp, a candle or flashlight could be used instead.)
4. When each person has found three things, the containers are placed on the table, and everyone tries to guess the story that each collection of objects represents.
5. When all the stories have been guessed, everyone returns the objects they chose to their proper places, and the game can be repeated.

Other ideas:

- Play this game outside in a park or woodland, although this may limit the kinds of objects you may be able to find.
- If you are on a beach, each person could create a sand sculpture of a scene from a Bible story. Then everyone can tour the sculptures and try to guess which stories are being represented.
- If you are having a church picnic, you could adapt this idea for an after-picnic activity. In advance, invite each family attending the picnic to bring along a few items from a Bible story of their choice. After the picnic, create the space for each family to arrange their objects. Number each collection clearly and give everyone a pencil and a piece of paper. Announce how many Bible story collections there are and ask people to write that many numbers down the left side of their paper. Then let them wander around the collections and try to guess which story the items represent. You could offer a prize for the most creative collection!

52

Bible-Name Acrostic Stories

THINGS YOU NEED:

- Pencils
- Paper

What you do:

1. Write a list of well-known people in the Bible.
2. Give each person in the group one of the names.
3. Ask them to write each letter of the name down the left-hand side of their paper.
4. Then invite them to make up a description of the person using the letters of their name as an acrostic. No other extra words are allowed!

   For example:

   Abraham

   A

   Brave

   Radical

   Abandons

   Home

   And

   Moves

Some of these descriptions can be quite amusing!

This activity can be repeated as often as you like.

Other ideas:

- Give everyone the same name and see who can come up with the most amusing or interesting acrostic description.
- Collect these mini-acrostics in a notebook.

53

Bible-Promise Search

THINGS YOU NEED:

- Bibles
- Concordance
- Pencils
- Small filing cards or slips of paper

What you do:

1. Give each person three cards or slips of paper.
2. On each piece of paper or card, ask them to write a short description of a person or situation that is in need of some spiritual encouragement, such as
   - a young mother who is feeling very tired
   - a teenager facing an important test at school
   - a young person being pressured to drink alcohol
   - someone who is feeling very lonely
   - a husband whose wife is very sick
3. Take the cards back and shuffle them well. Share them among the group.
4. Invite each person to try to search for a Bible text that will bring comfort and encouragement to the person or situation described on his card and to write them on the reverse of the card.
5. When you have finished, read out loud the situations and the corresponding promises.

Other ideas:

- Take one situation at a time and each try to search for appropriate promises. See how many different ones you find for each situation.
- Are there any people you know who are in these situations? How could you share the promises you have discovered with them? How else could you encourage them and help them in a practical way to bear their burdens? Sabbath is a day for supporting one other; is there anything you could do right away?

Bible Video-Clip Quiz

This game adds a new twist to watching Bible videos on Sabbath.

THINGS YOU NEED:

- A Bible video or DVD
- Pencils
- Paper

What you do:

1. Watch a Bible story video together.
2. As you watch, write down lots of different questions based on the video, such as colors of specific objects, what was happening in the background of the video at a particular time, how many people were in certain scenes, and what different people said. Try to be creative about the questions and pay attention to small details that could easily be missed.
3. Ask each other the questions and find out who is the most observant person in the family!

Other ideas:

- Parents could watch the video first and make up questions for the children.
- Show five-minute clips from several different videos instead of watching only one video.
- Use this kind of quiz for nature videos.
- Instead of using videos, read a short passage from the Bible or another book and then ask questions based on the story.

55

Bible-Verse Race

THINGS YOU NEED:

- Bibles (the same version for each person)

What you do:

1. Take turns reading from the Bible without giving any references.
2. The others in the group try to find the passage that the first person is reading. When someone finds the passage, he begins to read in unison with the first reader.
3. Continue doing this until everyone has found the Scripture passage and has joined in with the reading.

56

Rainbow "Thank You" Search

This game is suitable for quite young children.

THINGS YOU NEED:
- A separate piece of paper for each color of the rainbow—red, orange, yellow, green, blue, indigo, and violet

What you do:
1. Send your child on a scavenger hunt around the home to find things that are the different colors of the rainbow.
2. Try to encourage them to find things that God has made or that represent things that you could thank God for. For example, red could be for an apple that God has made for us, but it could also be for a toy fire engine which could represent how God takes care of us in emergencies.
3. When you have arranged everything on the table, give thanks to God for all the colorful things He has made and given to us.

Other ideas:
- Create a rainbow book of thanks with your child. Make a book with rainbow colored pages. Find pictures of things that are the different colors of the rainbow to glue on the page of the corresponding color. This could be added to over several months and could make a good wet-weather Sabbath activity.
- Do this activity outside and search for items in nature that match the seven colors of the rainbow.
- Follow the activity with a rainbow picnic or meal, where you try to eat something red, then orange, then yellow, and green, etc. Or make a rainbow fruit salad for supper that contains fruits of all the different colors of the rainbow and thank God for the beauty, colors, and flavors of the fruits.

57

Bible-Name Chain

THINGS YOU NEED:

- A small, soft ball or a rolled up sock

What you do:
1. Stand or sit in a circle.
2. One person starts by saying the name of a Bible character.
3. Then that person throws the ball gently to another person in the group.
4. The second person has to say the name of a Bible character that begins with the last letter of the first name that was said. For example: If the first person said "Elizabeth," the second person could say "Herod" because *H* is the last letter of the name *Elizabeth*.
5. Continue as long as you can and try not to repeat any of the names. You will soon find that many names end in *N* and *H,* and it becomes harder and harder to find new names beginning with these letters!

Other ideas:
- Play this game with Bible place names, with things that God has created, with animals, or with other Bible topics.
- Play this game outdoors.

58

Bible-Categories Quiz

THINGS YOU NEED:

- Pencils
- Paper
- Letters from a word game, either a pack of letter cards face down on a table or tiles in a small colored bag, so that they can be selected without being seen. If you have neither, just write each letter of the alphabet on a small piece of paper and pop all the letters in a bag.
- A kitchen timer or other method of counting three minutes

What you do:

1. First, invite each person in the group to think of a suitable Bible or nature category, such as Bible place names, animals in the Bible, foods mentioned in the Bible, flowers, or things made from water (such as fountains, streams, and dew).
2. List these categories down the left-hand side of a piece of lined or ruled paper.
3. Select a letter from the pile or bag and set the timer for three minutes.
4. See how many items you can list in the categories you have selected, beginning with the letter that has been chosen.
5. This can be done individually or as a group, and you can limit the answers to one per category or see how many you can find.

59

Bible-Object Creations

THINGS YOU NEED:

- Play-Doh modeling compound, or make your own (see recipe below)
- And /or Lego plastic building blocks
- And/or plain paper and pencils
- Blank index cards
- Pens

You will also need a list of different things mentioned in the Bible. If you have quite young children, include some easy ones for them. For example, the list could include the ark of the covenant, Joseph's coat of many colors, the manger that Jesus slept in, the lost sheep, Esther's crown, five loaves and two fishes, the widow's offering, Aaron's rod, and Moses' basket.

Write these items on the separate file cards, shuffle them, and place them face down on the table.

What you do:

1. One person draws a card from the stack and then tries to make a model from the modeling compound or the building blocks, or tries to draw a picture of the item named on the card.
2. The others try to guess which item from the Bible is being created.
3. The person drawing or creating is not allowed to say anything except "Yes" or "No" in response to questions.
4. When one item has been guessed, the next person takes a card.

Modeling Compound Recipe

2 cups all-purpose flour
I cup salt
2 tablespoons oil
2 cups water
2 teaspoons cream of tartar (This is important for helping preserve the dough.)
Food coloring (optional)

Combine all ingredients in a heavy cooking pan. Heat gently and stir until the mixture turns gooey. As soon as the mixture starts to come away from the sides of the pan, it's ready. It's important to cook this mixture just right, or it will be too runny or too stiff. Knead well, and then leave to cool. If stored in a plastic bag inside an airtight container, the modeling compound will last for months.

60

Proverbial Presentations

THINGS YOU NEED:
- Bibles, preferably a modern translation
- You may also need other art materials or props

What you do:
1. Select one chapter from the book of Proverbs.
2. Working as individuals or as groups, choose one of the verses in the chapter to illustrate as a poster, mini-drama, mime, display of objects, poem, rap, or short song.
3. Allow about fifteen to twenty minutes for each person or group to prepare their impromptu presentation.
4. Invite each person or group to make their presentation. After each presentation, everyone else has to try to guess which verse in the chapter was being presented. This stimulates creativity and an understanding of the wisdom of the Proverbs.

Other ideas:
- Try this idea with verses from the Psalms, the Beatitudes, 1 Corinthians 13, or portions of the Epistles.
- Your presentation ideas could form the basis of a creative church program.

CHAPTER 7

Exploring the Bible

Sabbath is a space for us to spend time creatively exploring the Bible. Here are some ideas to enrich your study of the Scriptures. Most of these activities can be used by older children, teens, and adults, and some ideas for adapting the activity for younger children have been included.

For more ideas for creative Bible activities for younger children, you might like to explore the book *100 Quick and Easy Worship Ideas for Kids,* Karen Holford, (Pacific Press, 2004).

- Spiritual Postcards
- Wordless Scriptures
- Letters From the Bible
- Refreshed Parables
- Scripture Sculptures
- Creative Characters
- God's Names
- Rainbow Promise Books
- Scripture Calligraphy
- Bible Scenes

61

Spiritual Postcards

Creating postcards in response to the Scriptures we are studying is a creative way of helping us to crystallize our ideas about a text or concept and to share these ideas with others. The postcards also provide a graphic illustrating our response to the Scriptures at different times. You don't have to be artistic because simpler images are often the most thought provoking.

THINGS YOU NEED:

- Bibles
- Selection of postcards to give you some ideas of the kind of artwork and designs that work on this small scale
- Postcard-sized pieces of white card or blank index cards
- Marker pens
- Pencils
- Crayons
- Scissors
- Collage materials (a variety of papers, fabrics, threads, glitter, etc.)
- Glue
- Watercolor paints and brushes

What you do:

1. Choose a passage of Scripture and read it carefully.
2. Invite each person to spend time quietly focusing on one of the texts or on a concept in the Bible passage.
3. Think about how you might illustrate that verse or concept on a postcard.
4. Use the various materials and tools to create a postcard-sized piece of artwork. You can draw, cut, layer papers, introduce 3-D concepts, and make collages to express your ideas. Or you could use computer graphics and a digital camera to create the image you have in mind.
5. When you have finished creating your postcards, show them to each other and say what inspired you to create that postcard and any insights you gained from creating the postcard. How did your ideas about the verse or concept change as you created the card, and how did creating the card help to develop your ideas about the text?
6. Find a way to display the cards together. Perhaps they could be mounted on a board or made into an album.

62

Wordless Scriptures

How would you convey some of the ideas in the Bible to someone who did not share your language? Or your culture? Or your faith?

THINGS YOU NEED:

- Bibles

What you do:

1. Choose a passage of Scripture and give each person a text to explore.
2. Invite each person to find a way to convey the message or meaning to someone who does not speak the same language you speak. What would you do? Perhaps you could draw something, use visual images, use your five senses, or use movement and gesture to convey the meaning.
3. Spend some time practicing your gestures or working on how you will convey your ideas.
4. Then show what you have created to each other. Can the others understand your meaning? How might you change your gestures to convey a clearer message?
5. Talk together about how you can share your faith with the people in your city who have no knowledge of God or the Bible.

Other ideas:

- Make an arrangement of objects or pictures to illustrate the text or concept rather than using gestures.
- For young children, choose simple texts and work together as a family to develop the actions for a Bible verse.

Letters From the Bible

If a character in the Bible were to write a letter to you today, what would they write to you? How would he or she inspire and encourage you?

THINGS YOU NEED:

- Bibles
- Plain paper
- A few sheets of special writing paper
- Pen

What you do:

1. Think about a character in the Bible whose experience might parallel yours in some way.
2. Read about their life and dilemmas and how God inspired them to manage their situation or provided help for them.
3. Imagine that character writing a letter to you today, to inspire you in the challenges you are facing. What might they write to encourage you today?
4. On a plain piece of paper, write the letter you imagine they might have written to you. When the letter is finished, you might like to rewrite it on the special writing paper or use a computer to print it neatly in a special font.
5. How has creating this letter made a difference to the way in which you see your situation? What has this exercise helped you to understand more about how God might view your current situation?

Other ideas:

- Younger children might like to make a card that a Bible character might have sent to them.
- It may be easier for children to write a letter from themselves to God or to a Bible character, instead of having to think about how someone else might write to them.
- Or, if they were to make a trophy for a Bible character, what would the trophy be for, what would it look like, and who would they give it to?

64

Refreshed Parables

If Jesus were to tell His parables in your community today, how would they be different from the ones He told in Bible times?

THINGS YOU NEED:

- Bibles
- Pens
- Paper

What you do:

1. Choose a favorite Bible story or one that seems particularly relevant to your community today.
2. Consider how the story or parable would unfold in your community. How would the story be different? If you were to write it as a current news item or a story told in your local dialect or culture, how might it be written?
3. Work together or individually to rewrite the parable as Jesus may have told it today.
4. If you have worked separately, read your "refreshed" parables to each other to see how they are different or similar.
5. Talk together about how rewriting the parable for today has developed your understanding of their application to your life and community.

Another idea:

- Use these refreshed parables as the basis of a poem, rap, mime, or drama, depending on what is appropriate and acceptable in your culture.

65

Scripture Sculptures

Creating something out of paper can help us to focus on different aspects of the Scriptures.

THINGS YOU NEED:

- Bibles
- Plain white paper

What you do:

1. Choose a passage from the Bible, such as a psalm, proverb, or parable.
2. Divide the passage into portions, and give each person a verse and a piece of paper to sculpt into something representative of that verse. The sculpture can be very simple, and the paper can be torn, folded, or scrunched into any shape.
3. Allow five to ten minutes per sculpt and then invite each person to read their verse, to show their sculpture, and then to tell what insights they gained as they created their object.
4. Make an arrangement of the sculptures and their texts.

Other ideas:

- Instead of paper, use Play-Doh modeling compound. See the recipe under "Bible-Object Creations" in the "Almost-Instant Bible Games" chapter.
- If you are outside, use stones or sticks instead of paper to create your sculptures.
- On a beach, use sand and shells to create the sculptures.
- Try doing this activity for 1 Corinthians 13:4–8, and make a sculpture to illustrate various aspects of love. Perhaps you could sculpt or create hearts from various materials that illustrate various aspects of love, such as patience, kindness, respect, or forgiveness.
- Children might like to create scenes from Bible stories out of modeling compound or toy bricks and construction kits, or as a diorama in a shoe box.

66

Creative Characters

Reflecting on a Bible story from the perspectives of the different characters involved can make a story come alive and can help you dig deeper into the ideas within the story.

THINGS YOU NEED:

- Bibles
- Pens
- Paper

What you do:
1. Choose a Bible story together that has enough different characters for everyone in the group to choose a different person. In large groups, give each group a person to discuss. Consider the birth of Jesus, the stories of some of His miracles, His parables, or even the Last Supper, the Crucifixion, or the Resurrection.
2. Give each person or group enough time to read the story together and to think about the story from the perspective of the character they have selected or been assigned. How might this person have been feeling at various points in the story? What might they have been happy or sad about? What might have been their fears or their hopes? Why might they have done or said the things they did? What might they have learned from their experiences in this story? As you have reflected on this character, what have you learned about God's love for this character and for you?
3. Pool your ideas to create a soliloquy or monologue (these are words spoken by a character as if they are his or her own thoughts and not necessarily heard by the others in the scene). The soliloquy can be quite short. A few sentences will be adequate, but you can write more if you wish.
4. Then take turns reading aloud the various thoughts and ideas inspired by each person in the Bible story.
5. If you want to be more dramatic, you could create a simple scene and invite each character to stand up and speak in turn, while the others are silent and still.

Another idea:
- Develop and refine this idea into a presentation for a church service or program. People could practice their speeches, wear appropriate clothing, and come "alive" and speak their part when a spotlight shines on them. Music could be chosen or created to accompany the presentation.

God's Names

God has many names, and they reflect many of the facets of His character and personality. Often we focus on only a few of His many amazing qualities.

THINGS YOU NEED:

- Bibles
- Pens
- Paper
- Bible encyclopedia and concordance
- Or visit <www.lillyofthevalleyva.com/jesuslovesyou-godsnames-complist. html> or search the Internet for other sites that list the names of God

What you do:

1. First, list all the names of God that you can remember from the Bible.
2. Write each of the names of God on a separate piece of paper. You might like to look in the Bible encyclopedia or on a Web site to find other names of God that you might have forgotten or not be aware of. If you are doing this activity with children, use the names of God that they can relate to, such as God the Father, God the Shepherd, and God the Creator.
3. Pass the sheets of paper around the group and give each person a few moments to consider what it means to them that God is a Father, Shepherd, Creator, etc. Invite them to write any comments, reflections, sentence prayers, or praise words about that specific name of God. When each person has written on one sheet of paper, the papers with God's names and the reflections are passed to the left and each person is given a new one to consider and respond to.
4. As the sheets are passed around, it is interesting to read what other people have written.
5. You might also like to look up texts about that name of God and add other ideas from the Scriptures to the sheets of paper.

Other ideas:

- Place sheets of paper with some of the different names of God around the walls of the room and let people wander from one to the other, reflecting on the names and adding any comments or responses that they wish to make.
- Create a notebook of different names of God and the responses of your family members to the names of God. This could form the basis of an ongoing project in which your family can explore the names of God and who God is.
- Children could help create a scrapbook of God's names or character traits and add their own ideas about God, as well as pictures they have collected or drawn.

68

Rainbow Promise Books

This is a colorful way to introduce children to God's many promises.

THINGS YOU NEED:

- Bibles
- Concordance
- Sheets of colored paper in all the colors of the rainbow (red, orange, yellow, green, blue, indigo, and violet)
- Sheets of white paper
- Staples and stapler
- Colored and sparkling gel ink pens

What you do:

1. Stack colored pages in the order listed above, from red to violet. Put a piece of white paper on the top and bottom of the pile of paper and staple the long sides together to make a book. Title the book "God's Promises."
2. On each colored page write a matching title as listed below:

Red	Promises to save us
Orange	Promises to bring us happiness
Yellow	Promises to protect us
Green	Promises to provide for our needs
Blue	Promises to refresh us and renew our strength
Indigo	Promises to heal us
Violet	Promises to bring us peace

3. Search the Bible for promises and write them on the page where they fit the category. If you find promises that don't fit one of these categories, write them inside the front and back covers. Use the colored pens to write the promises on the pages.
4. Encourage your child to add to the book as they find new promises.

Other ideas:

- Find a notebook with rainbow-colored pages and write a promise on each page, according to the categories listed above.
- Make a promise box, using different colored cards for different kinds of promises.
- Use different colored highlighter pens to mark the promises as you find them in your Bible.

Scripture Calligraphy

You don't have to be an expert at calligraphy to enjoy making the Scriptures look beautiful.

THINGS YOU NEED:

- Pencils
- Rulers
- A variety of different colored gel ink pens or other interesting pens, but not ball point pens
- A variety of writing papers with different textures and finishes, or even good quality tracing paper or other translucent papers
- Computer and printer (optional)

What you do:

1. Choose a Scripture verse or passage that is special to you.
2. Read it through carefully and slowly and consider some different ways in which you could write the passage to illustrate its meaning in some way. For example, you can write the words in different colors, different fonts, or different shapes. For example, write 1 Corinthians 13 inside a heart shape, either from left to right, as usual, or in a spiral from the outside of the heart to the center.
3. It is worth planning your calligraphy on scrap paper before you start on the special paper, so you can check your spacing, sizes, and shapes, etc.
4. If you don't feel confident writing on special paper, experiment with computer fonts and colors and different tools for transforming fonts, and create your design on the computer instead.
5. Collect your Scripture calligraphy projects in an album and decorate the pages with scrap-booking supplies to suit the themes of the texts.

Other ideas:

- Use your piece of calligraphy to decorate a greeting card to send to someone. You can photocopy your calligraphy to make cards for special occasions or even a bulletin cover for church or for a wedding or another event.
- Children's writing has a charm all its own! You could invite your children to write out and decorate twelve different texts and use their designs on a do-it-yourself blank calendar to give as a gift to a grandparent.
- Scan the designs into your computer and adapt them to decorate T-shirts, cards, posters, etc.

70

Bible Scenes

This is an interesting way to explore a Bible story, especially good for those Sabbaths when you don't want to go outside!

THINGS YOU NEED:

- Bibles
- All kinds of props that you have around the home—be inventive and creative!
- A vivid imagination

What you do:

1. Choose a Bible story and read it together.
2. Re-create a scene from the story in your home with things you already have. Invite your child to help you create the scene, and let yourself become a child along with her so that you use your imagination and playfulness as well! You could try one of these:
   - Jonah in the whale (the space under a table covered with dark blankets or sheets) What else might be in there with you?
   - Jesus at the Last Supper
   - Gathering manna in the desert outside your tent (Popcorn makes good manna!)
   - Esther in the palace (a lovely activity for little girls who like to dress up)
   - Joseph in prison
   - Samuel in the temple
   - Your home in heaven

There are as many possibilities as your imagination will allow!

Another idea:

- Wear clothes similar to those worn in Bible times and eat food that people in Bible times might have eaten. Learn all you can about life in Bible times and the flavors, smells, sights, and sounds of life then that you could re-create today.

CHAPTER 8

Family-Building Activities

Sabbath is a day for strengthening family relationships. Here are some ideas for building your spiritual closeness as a family.

- Spiritual Family Tree
- Answered-Prayer Stories
- Spiritual-Gift Boxes
- Dream, Help, Love, Smile
- Family Altars
- Family Advertisements
- Thank-You Cards
- Family Blessings
- Family Life Journeys
- Family-Faith Collage

71

Spiritual Family Tree

It is important for children to know their spiritual heritage. Telling the stories about how faith has been transmitted through generations in your family can be a bonding and encouraging experience. It can also be useful to tell the stories of those people who chose not to follow God or who chose different spiritual pathways.

THINGS YOU NEED:
- A large piece of plain paper (or stick several sheets of paper together to make a larger sheet)
- Pens
- Repositionable sticky notes

What you do:
1. First, write the names of every person in your child's family, for as many generations as you are aware, on separate sticky notes.
2. Arrange these sticky notes on the large piece of paper to create a family tree. Once all the names are laid out neatly, with enough space, you might like to draw the family tree on the large piece of paper.
3. Then, choosing one person at a time, tell what you know about their spiritual journey, such as how they became a Christian, what their spiritual gifts might have been, how God worked in their lives, and any stories of special spiritual significance. If both of your child's parents are present, take turns telling stories from each side of the family.
4. Write brief spiritual histories on sticky notes and stick them on the different people's names.

Other ideas:
- Refine your family tree and draw it as attractively as you can. Add people's photos if you have them.
- Write the stories of people's spiritual journeys in an attractive book, so that they can be passed on to future generations.
- Write the stories on your computer, decorate them with appropriate images, and print copies for family members to keep.

72

Answered-Prayer Stories

Hearing how prayers have been answered in your family can be an inspiring and faith-encouraging activity.

THINGS YOU NEED:
- You might like to capture these stories in a notebook or as sound recordings.

What you do:

Taking turns, tell as many stories of answered prayer as you can remember. Often there are many everyday stories of answered prayers, such as lost items being found, people being healed, or other ways in which God answered prayers to bless or guide you.

Another idea:
- Start a notebook of answered prayers and add answers whenever you notice them. Perhaps your child could illustrate the book with drawings of these answers.

73

Spiritual-Gift Boxes

As a family, we may be more aware of each other's spiritual gifts than others might be. This family-building activity is a lovely way of affirming each other's spiritual gifts.

THINGS YOU NEED:

- A list of spiritual gifts from the Bible (Look in Romans 12:6–8; I Corinthians 12:27–30; and Ephesians 4:11–13.)
- A small, attractive gift box for each person in the family, chosen to suit each person's taste
- Paper or thin card, cut into shapes to fit inside the gift boxes
- Pens

What you do:

1. Label each gift box with someone's name, and place the boxes in the middle of the table.
2. On a piece of card, write a spiritual gift, talent, or special quality that you have noticed in a person's life and place that card in his or her gift box. You can add more than one card to someone's box, and you need to add at least one thing to each person's gift box.
3. When everyone has written all the gifts, qualities, and talents that they have recognized in the other family members' lives and placed them in the correct boxes, each box is given to the person whose name is on the label.
4. Take time for each person to open his box and to reflect on what he finds inside. You may need to read aloud the cards for younger children and help them with writing their cards. Even small children have spiritual gifts and talents that need to be recognized, used, and nurtured.
5. Have a time of prayerful thanks for all the gifts, talents, and qualities that God has given to your family members.

Other ideas:

- Give each person a plain gift box that they can decorate for themselves.
- Fill the gift boxes with cards thanking God for all the good things He has done for your family and given to you.

74

Dream, Help, Love, Smile

This positive activity can build understanding and communication in a family.

THINGS YOU NEED:
- Paper
- Pencils
- Crayons
- Marker pens

What you do:
1. Fold the pieces of paper in half and in half again so that when the page is opened again it has been divided into four quarters.
2. In each of the quarters draw and write one of the following things:

The outline of a cloud	A dream I have is . . .
The outline of a hand	Something I could use some help with this week is . . .
The outline of a heart	Something that makes me feel really loved is . . .
A smiley face	Something that made me happy this week was . . .

   You should end up with a different drawing and sentence starter in each quarter. You could create one of these by hand or on a computer and make as many copies as you need.
3. Give a copy to each person and invite them to finish the sentences on their sheet of paper.
4. When you have all finished, show what you have done and read out your completed sentences. Then ask how you can support each other to fulfill the dreams, help each other during the following week, and make each other to feel loved. Celebrate together about whatever made each person happy.

Other ideas:
- Cut the shapes out of various colored paper and write on each shape, instead of folding the paper into quarters. Clouds—light blue; hands—your family's skin color; hearts—pink; smiles—yellow.
- Swap hearts, clouds, smiles, and hands with each other and promise to do one thing in the following week to encourage every person toward their dreams, to show them love, to make them smile, or to help them.

75

Family Altars

In Bible times families would build stone altars to commemorate God's deliverance and protection. Today we can build miniature altars for similar purposes.

THINGS YOU NEED:

- Flat stones of all shapes and sizes (Flat stones stack better and stay where you put them.)
- Plain white plates on which to arrange the stones
- Strong adhesive (optional)

What you do:
1. Place a pile of stones in the middle of the group.
2. Invite each person to choose some stones and arrange them to represent God's guidance or protection in the family or your family's experience at the moment. Small children can choose one stone per person in the family and arrange them however they wish, or make other patterns and shapes with the stones.

Other ideas:
- To commemorate a special event, create a stone shape or miniature altar and glue the stones together to create a permanent stone sculpture, or you could photograph your stone creation. In Bible times, these altars were given names that gave some idea of their history, and you could name your altars, too.
- Write words on the stones with permanent ink, telling the story of God's care or answered prayers.

76

Family Advertisements

God has made every family different. What is unique and special about your family?

THINGS YOU NEED:

- Paper
- Art materials
- Possibly a computer with a graphics program

What you do:

1. Invite each person in the family to create a poster to advertise your family. You will need to think about how God has made your family unique, the special qualities your family has, and the unusual things your family does.
2. You might like to base your poster around a current promotional advertisement, adapted to suit your family. If you are skilled with graphics, you can cut and paste different images to adapt advertising posters and slogans.

Other ideas:

- Instead of creating individual posters, create one big poster together.
- Create a slogan that advertises your family.
- Take the letters in your surname and create a funny slogan in which each word begins with one of the letters in your surname. For example, Holford:

     Happy
     Ones
     Loving
     Fun
     On
     Rainy
     Days

77

Thank-You Cards

Say "Thank You" to God in a special way for all He has done for your family.

THINGS YOU NEED:
- Purchased or home-made Thank-you cards
- Pens

What you do:
1. You can create your own cards if you wish or print some using your computer. Purchased cards are fine too.
2. Give each person a Thank-you card and invite them to write a Thank-You note to God for all He has done for your family in the past week.
3. Read the cards out to each other and display them.

Other ideas:
- Collect the Thank-you cards in an album or scrapbook.
- Write a Thank-You card from your family once a month and continue to add to the collection of cards over the years. It can be very encouraging to reread them.
- Use one Thank-you card and let everyone write in the same card.
- Create a huge Thank-You poster or bulletin board and add all kinds of Thank-You messages for God to the board whenever you wish.
- Write Thank-you cards to each other, showing appreciation for the things each person does to help and support the family.

78

Family Blessings

A beautiful tradition that has been lost in our times is the tradition of blessing each other.

THINGS YOU NEED:
- A small bottle of scented oil or olive oil
- Ideas for blessings (or write your own)

The LORD bless you and keep you;
the LORD make his face to shine upon you
and be gracious to you;
the LORD turn his face toward you
and give you peace
(Numbers 6:25).

May grace of the Lord Jesus Christ, and the love of God,
and the fellowship of the Holy Spirit be with you
(2 Corinthians 13:14).

May God himself, the God of peace, sanctify you through and through.
May your whole spirit, soul and body be kept blameless
at the coming of our Lord Jesus Christ
(1 Thessalonians 5:23).

What you do:
On Sabbath bless each other by saying a Sabbath blessing over each other as you lay your hand on their heads or hands, or as you "anoint" them with a drop of oil on their foreheads or hands. This can be a powerful and quietly sacred experience.

Other ideas:
- Say a blessing over someone as you sprinkle them with flower petals. You can use scented fabric petals that will last for years, and you can revive their fragrance by adding a few drops of essential oil to the petals before sealing them in a plastic bag for a few days.
- Writing your own blessings is also a very significant act to offer others, especially when the blessing is linked to a life event, such as a birthday, baptism, or leaving home.

79

Family Life Journeys

Making a map of a family's life journey can be an interesting way of seeing how God has been leading in the life of a family.

THINGS YOU NEED:

- Large piece of paper
- Colored marker pens
- Bible with a map of Paul's or Abraham's travels, or the wanderings of the children of Israel in the wilderness

What you do:

1. Look at the maps of the routes Paul, Abraham, or the Israelites took on their journeys.
2. Talk about your own spiritual journey as a family. What were the desert times, the lush valleys, the high mountains, the bumpy road experiences, the dead ends, etc?
3. Work together to create a map of your spiritual journey and the spiritual landscape along the way.

Other ideas:

- Each person could create her own spiritual map to show to each other.
- Discuss questions such as these: Where would you like your journey to go in the future? Where is God calling you to next? How will you get there? What do you hope will be there?

80

Family-Faith Collage

This activity creates a collection of things that represent different aspects of your family and faith. Symbols of faith experiences have been very important to believers down through the ages. The ark of the covenant contained items that were of spiritual significance to the children of Israel, such as Aaron's rod, manna, and the Ten Commandments.

THINGS YOU NEED:
- Bibles
- Pens and paper, or words printed using a computer
- A collection of items that represent different aspects of your family
- A shadow box, box frame suitable for a 3-D collage, or other kind of container in which your items can be displayed permanently or semi-permanently

What you do:
1. Invite each person to think about your family and your experience of faith.
2. Jot down words that describe your family's faith experience, your unique rituals, your answered prayers, your approach to God's love and grace, your concept of Sabbath and creation, etc.
3. Using these ideas as a basis, hunt for objects that convey some of these concepts and experiences. Here are some ideas of objects collected by one family:
   - Sunflower seeds to represent the growth of faith within the family
   - A small candle to represent the family's desire to be a witness in their community
   - A key to remind them of how God helped them find a good home to live in
   - Some natural-colored wool to represent their desire to follow Jesus, the Good Shepherd
   - A button shaped like a treble clef to represent how the family enjoyed singing worship songs together

Favorite texts, connected with the objects, were printed on strips of paper, which were then torn carefully and woven and twisted between the objects.

These items were arranged and glued in a small display frame to create a picture for the family's living room, where they have their worships.

Other ideas:
- Each person could create their own small collage, or families could create a faith collage each year to illustrate stages in their spiritual journey.
- Families could gather items together, discuss them, photograph the collection, and then return the objects to their usual places.

CHAPTER 9

Sabbath Crafting Ideas

Sabbath is a celebration of God's creation. He has also given human beings an amazing capacity to be creative in ways that honor Him and share His love.

Some families find that being creative together can be a way of connecting with each other and with God in new and exciting ways.

Here are some craft projects that may add some simple creativity to your Sabbaths:

- Spiritual Scrapbooking
- Creating Cards
- Christian Craft Projects for Children
- Creating Mini-books
- Making Puppets
- Creating a City of God
- Creating Witness T-Shirts
- Sabbath Candle Lanterns
- Bible-Promise Boxes
- Ready-Made Bible Crafts

81

Spiritual Scrapbooking

Many families are currently interested in creating scrapbook albums of their family life. Scrapbook albums can also be created to tell your family's spiritual story, to log your prayer requests and answers, and to offer thanks and praise to God for special life events.

Scrapbooking can be as simple or as complex as you want to make it, and there are many books and Web sites that can show you all kinds of ideas and techniques. It is an ideal project for the entire family, becuase it can involve photography, computer skills, craft skills, and simple artwork from quite young children.

What to do:

You and your family can also create mini-albums themed around a passage of Scripture or the days of Creation, or themes such as gratitude, love, sharing, or grace. Choose pictures from the Internet (try exploring <www.gettyimages. com>, where you can search for and download excellent quality royalty-free images), or take your own photos as part of the project. Use your computer to print any text you want to include in the album and use your favorite graphics program to create stickers, other pictures, and decorative elements to add to the pages. You can use pressed flowers and leaves, cancelled postage stamps, old greeting cards, gift-wrap, and other decorative items to enhance the pages. There are many stores where you can buy all kinds of embellishments for the pages, and it is worth visiting these for ideas and to purchase resources.

Another idea:

• Keep the albums for your own collection and leave them on your coffee table for visitors to read, or make them as encouraging gifts to give away to special people.

Internet search words:

spiritual scrapbooking; faithbooking; scrapbooking

82

Creating Cards

Making greetings cards is another craft that can involve the whole family and can be as simple or as elaborate as your skills and resources will allow. You can create cards with messages and greetings that are spiritually encouraging. It can be so uplifting to receive a handmade card that contains a special message. You probably know many people who would be delighted to receive your cards, and the cards can also be used to share God's love with people in your friendship and neighborhood groups. You can read an explanation about how to use Christian cards as a ministry at <www.dayspring.com>.

What to do:

You can use your computer printer or your own unique handwriting to create the messages for your cards.

If you are not sure what to write in a card, explore the ecards at <www.dayspring.com> and <www.crosscards.com> for some beautiful and creative possibilities. If you have a greeting-card package on your computer, it may also contain spiritually encouraging verses that you can use for your homemade cards.

Use all kinds of craft items and skills to create interesting cards, trying to match the design to the words. Keep a box of ideas and bits and pieces that can help you to make the cards.

Many craft magazines have ideas for making simple cards and craft shops have rubber stamps, stickers, embossing stencils, and hundreds of ideas and resources for creating cards simply and cheaply. Visit your local library for books about making cards. Buy a set of blank cards and envelopes and pray for inspiration as you design, make, write, and send the cards.

Another idea:

- Make cards for your neighbors and include an invitation to come to your home for some simple refreshments and a time of getting to know each other.

Internet search words:

creating greetings cards; card-making; card crafts

83

Christian Craft Projects for Children

Children often learn about Bible stories while they are doing craft projects. The action of making something may help them to remember the lessons being taught. You could choose crafts that are linked with their current Bible lessons or with a Bible story video that you are planning to watch on Sabbath.

What to do:

Hundreds of Bible story crafts are available through an excellent Web site at <www.mssscrafts.com> maintained by a mother in Australia. From the home page you can easily find crafts related to almost every Bible story and links to many other Christian craft sites. There are printable patterns and instruction sheets, coloring pages, and puzzles. Also look for ideas at <www.daniellesplace.com>.

It can be helpful to keep a craft box for Sabbath craft projects, stocked with items such as paper plates, craft sticks, stickers, colored paper and cards, paints, marker pens, yarn, glitter, small boxes, scissors, and anything else you think may be useful. Try to choose the projects earlier in the week so you can check that you have everything you need for Sabbath.

For best results, work alongside your child because this builds her confidence and your relationship together. But also allow her space to develop her own creativity and for her own ideas to emerge and develop.

Other ideas:
- Give away some craft items as gifts of encouragement.
- Start a children's Sabbath craft club in your area.

Internet search words:

Christian crafts, children

84

Creating Mini-books

Making tiny books is a fascinating craft for children. Some patterns are fun and quite simple, and the books fold into accordion pleats or other unusual shapes. Children can use these tiny books to write special Bible verses or portions of the scripture that they are trying to memorize. Making an unusual book, writing on the pages, and decorating the pages to suit the words can be a lovely Sabbath project. Consider making a miniature book of the days of Creation, Psalm 23, 1 Corinthians 13, or your favorite Bible promises. Even small children can create their own simple Bible story books by drawing pictures on the pages. Grown-ups can take the time to make quite artistic and special books.

THINGS YOU NEED:
- Blank sheets of white paper
- Scissors
- Pens
- Coloring materials

What you do:
1. Fold the sheet of paper in half so that the long sides of the sheet of paper meet. Crease the sheet firmly along this central fold and leave the sheet folded.
2. Fold the paper in half again with the short sides meeting, and crease firmly again. Leave this fold in place and fold the piece of paper again, with the new short side meeting the other short side.
3. Open the page and refold, matching short side to short side so the page is folded in half across the center. Take a pair of scissors and cut along the fold line that runs from the center toward the short edge, but only cut as far as the next crease. This will give you a sheet of paper with a slit in the middle of it, parallel with the long side.
4. Open out the page again and fold it in half with the long sides meeting, and hold it so that the crease is at the top. Bring each end of the cut slit to meet in the middle, so that a top view of the paper creates an X shape. This can then be folded around to make a small booklet with a front and back cover and six small pages inside.

Other ideas:
- Look in library books for other ideas for making and decorating miniature books. Most book-making supplies are inexpensive, so you don't have to

84

worry if something doesn't work out as planned.

- If you become more adventurous, you could create simple pop-up books of Bible stories. Who knows, maybe your unique book could become a best-seller!

- For some simple and interesting book patterns, visit <www.canby.com/ hockmanchupp/student_folder_websites.html>.

Internet search words:

creating miniature books; book making; book binding; making books for children; book-making supplies; making pop-up books; paper engineering

85

Making Puppets

As a family, create some simple puppets and a script to retell a Bible story. There are patterns for all kinds of puppets on <www.daniellesplace.com>, <familycrafts.about.com/od/puppets/> and <www.sagecraft.com/puppetry>.

THINGS YOU NEED:

- Patterns, instructions, and materials for making simple puppets (You can find patterns for simple puppets in the children's craft section of your local library.)

What you do:

1. Create the puppets according to the instructions, or improvise and make your own out of materials you can find in your home.
2. Choose a Bible story and encourage your child to create or write a script for a puppet play based on that Bible story. Make the puppets together to tell the story. Practice the story well, and it could be performed in church as a children's story or in Sabbath School, or it could be taken to a retirement or nursing home.
3. If your child has a quiet voice or is a little shy, it may be useful to let him record his script, so that he has to think only about the puppets while performing, and the sound of his voice can be amplified so that the audience can hear. You could even video the finished puppet performance!

Other ideas:

- Puppet scripts are also available and you may find these in books or online.
- If your family enjoys working with puppets, you may like to consider whether God is calling you to begin your own puppet ministry. You can purchase specially made puppets from <www.timetosow.com>, and you can also purchase CDs of scripts and music especially made for puppet ministries.

Internet search words:

Christian puppet ministry; Christian puppet scripts; Christian puppet music

86

Creating a City of God

This project may need a large space on the floor or on a table. It is also an ideal project to do as a group of families or as a unique church program.

THINGS YOU NEED:
- Colored papers
- Colored cards
- Colored foil
- Clear acetate
- Craft glue
- Scissors
- Paint
- Markers
- Colored tissue paper
- Colored modeling clay or dough
- Craft items such as craft sticks and chenille stems
- A roll of thick paper to create streets and a city plan
- Lots of small boxes or clean packaging items

What you do:
1. Read together Revelation 21 and 22 about what the City of God will be like in heaven.
2. Create your own imaginary City of God. Of course it will be very different from the real city, but that doesn't matter. The idea is to stimulate the imagination about heaven and how it might be different from life here on earth. What do we know will be there? What else do we imagine might be there? Think about your own city and what it contains. How might heaven be different or the same? How will people move around, find food, live, play, worship, work, create things, meet together, etc? What will the houses be like? What will children do? Will there be parks? Will there be money-free shops where people give away the beautiful things they have made? How will we worship God? Will there be a huge place we all meet together? Will there be worshipful banners in the streets and posters of God's words?
3. Have plenty of space for people to create the things that they think might be in the City of God. Make a large street layout and place the things on the streets. After a while look at the city together and discuss the following questions:
   - Why did you choose to make what you made? What's missing?
   - What else might there need to be in the City of God?
   - How will this city be different from the city where you live now?
   - What one thing could we do as a group to make our city a little bit more like the City of God?

Another idea:
- Use this activity to inspire your group to do something good for your city. Pray about your ideas, research them, and talk to the relevant city officials about your ideas and how best to approach the task you have in mind.

Creating Witness T-Shirts

The focus of this activity is to create T-shirts that can be worn as a witness for God.

THINGS YOU NEED:

- Some design ideas to help you stimulate your creativity. You might like to look at <www.religioustshirts.co.uk>.
- Plain white or colored T-shirts (These can be purchased cheaply and may even be available from a thrift store.)
- Computer printable T-shirt transfer paper
- Fabric paints, embellishments, stencils, etc., from a craft store

What you do:

1. Pray that God will inspire you as you design these T-shirts together.
2. What you do will depend upon the technique you choose for decorating your T-shirt because there are dozens of methods you could use. Some T-shirt decorating ideas are simple for quite young children. You can draw an outline with fabric crayons and let them color it in. Or you can stick a heart shape on the T-shirt and let your child scribble on the T-shirt with different colors. Then remove the heart and you will have a plain heart in the middle of lots of colors. Add a slogan to the heart with a fabric painting marker or dimensional paint.
3. Research in library books or on the Internet for T-shirt decorating ideas; check that you have all the equipment you need before you start to design the T-shirt.
4. If you have some simple computer skills, you can create designs on the computer that can easily be ironed onto the T-shirt. Follow the instructions on the packet and don't forget to reverse the image if you have words on your design. Even if you create a computer image for your T-shirt, you can still embellish it with buttons, dimensional fabric paint, glitter, and other decorations.
5. Make sure that any fabric paint is left to dry completely and that any paints that require fixing are fixed as necessary.
6. When washing the T-shirts, follow the laundry care instructions supplied by your craft products.
   Remember to wear the T-shirts as a witness! That's why you made them!

Another idea:

- If you don't want to make T-shirts, create designs for plain calico bags or wall hangings.

Internet search words:

T-shirt decorating crafts; Christian T-shirts

88

Sabbath Candle Lanterns

This simple craft can have lovely results, and it is suitable for quite small children. Older children can be more adventurous and find different ways of decorating their lanterns.

THINGS YOU NEED:

- Clean, empty, plain-sided glass jars
- Colored tissue paper
- White water-soluble glue diluted with a little water
- Paste brushes or thick paint brushes
- Glitter and stick-on gems (optional)
- Dimensional fabric paint (optional)
- Tea-lights or small votive candles
- Long matches or tapers for lighting the candles

What you do:

1. Paint the outside of the jar with the diluted glue.
2. While the glue is still wet, tear the tissue paper into pieces and stick it onto the jar. Do this until the sides of the jar are completely covered with tissue. Let dry.
3. Recoat the tissue and the jar with diluted glue as a protective layer and let dry again.
4. Add extra embellishments if you wish, such as glitter or dimensional paint, in swirls and flowers or any other shapes you like.
5. Let dry.
6. Add a tea-light or candle to the jar and light with a long match.
7. Turn out the lights and enjoy the lantern!

Do take adequate safety precautions with any lighted candles, and always blow them out before you leave the room.

Other ideas:

- Adults and older children might like to cover their jars with mulberry paper, or other delicate Japanese papers with interesting designs.
- These lanterns make good gifts to share with others.

89

Bible-Promise Boxes

This is another craft that can be as simple or as complicated as you wish, depending on the skills of the children and adults involved in the project.

THINGS YOU NEED:

- Bibles
- Bible concordance
- Assortment of small boxes, tiny bags, or baskets
- Things to decorate the boxes or bags, such as stickers and flowers
- Card stock blank business cards are a good size and shape, but you can cut the card into the size you want, or even into unusual shapes like hearts and flowers.
- Pens
- Crayons
- Scissors
- Glue

What you do:
1. Look through the Bible for your favorite promises. Many are found in the Gospels and in the psalms. Use the concordance to help you find other promises.
2. Write the promises on the cards and arrange them in the container you have chosen.
3. Add to these at any time to build up your own collection of promises. On the back of the promise cards, you might like to write how God fulfilled that promise in your life or in your family.

Other ideas:
- Make Bible promise boxes to give as gifts.
- Use the computer to print a selection of promises onto the cards, if you are making lots of boxes to give away.

90

Ready-Made Bible Crafts

A wide variety of Christian craft kits are available at your local Christian book store. You can even purchase a CD-ROM from American Greetings (Sunday School Crafts) that contains Christian crafts to print and use, including mobiles, bookmarks, booklets, sun catchers, and T-shirt designs, plus lots more.

What to do:
1. Check discount book stores for press-out kits to make items such as Noah's ark and houses from Bible times, or to find rubber-stamping kits with Christian themes. You may also find kits to make origami animals, so that you can create an origami Garden of Eden or Noah's ark. It can be surprising what you can find when you search hard enough.
2. Your local craft store may also have kits suitable for Sabbath, to make nature-themed items, nativity sets, rainbow sun-catchers, etc.
3. Check out your local library for craft books. In the children's section, you will find books of things to make from all over the world that can be used to help your child explore mission lands. Other children's craft books often have simple patterns and instructions for making animal and nature items that can be adapted for use on Sabbath.
4. Be willing to explore, take your time, and be creative—and you will soon find ways of adapting crafts to make projects that are suitable for Sabbath.

CHAPTER 10

Music, Mime, and Drama Activities

Using music to praise and worship God is a Sabbath activity that dates back for centuries. Today there are even more ways to use music to worship God and to develop our relationship with Him. Movement, mime, acting, and visual images can also be used to illustrate songs and Bible stories and can help us find fresh meanings in familiar words.

- Musical Scriptures
- The Hum Game
- Write Your Own Praise Song
- Scrapbook of Songs
- Making Your Own Instruments
- Hymn and Song Stories
- Musical Mimes
- Sound Scriptures
- Christian Drama
- Illustrated Songs

91

Musical Scriptures

Today many movies, advertisements, and TV programs have their own theme music and soundtracks to set the atmosphere. This activity gives you the opportunity to choose a soundtrack for your favorite passages of Scripture.

THINGS YOU NEED:
- CDs, MP3s, or cassettes of instrumental music (without words)
- Machine for playing the music
- Bibles

What you do:
1. Choose a scripture passage that is meaningful to you. It could be as simple as the Lord's Prayer or Psalm 23, 103, or 139—whatever you like. Many of the psalms are especially good for setting to music because they were written as songs.
2. Match your chosen portion of Scripture to a piece of music that you like and that you think suits the passage you have chosen.
3. Play the music as you read the scripture passage aloud and check that its mood matches the words you are reading.
4. Play your musical Scriptures to each other and tell why you chose the music and Scriptures to go together.

Other ideas:
- If you are musical, write your own music to accompany the scripture passage you have chosen.
- Even if you don't play an instrument, you can improvise with humming, simple home-made instruments, and even body percussion to accompany the Scriptures.

92

The Hum Game

Often we recognize many more tunes than we can name!

THINGS YOU NEED:

- People who can hum
- Possibly some hymn or worship song books to give you some ideas in case you have "hummer's block"!

What you do:
1. One person begins to hum a tune.
2. Everyone else tries to guess the name of the hymn or the first line of the song.
3. When the song has been correctly identified, the next person hums a tune.

Another idea:
- Instead of guessing the name of the hymn, any person who recognizes the tune could hum along as soon as they think they have guessed correctly, until everyone is humming together.

93

Write Your Own Praise Song

The psalmist tells us over and over in his psalms to sing a new song to the Lord! Making up your own song is a great way of being sure that your song is a new one!

THINGS YOU NEED:

- Bibles
- Perhaps some music manuscript paper. You can print blank sheet music from <www.blanksheetmusic.net> or search the Internet for other free printable music manuscripts.
- Pencils

What you do:

1. First, write the lyrics. They don't have to rhyme or even have a certain number of beats in each line. You might like to take a psalm from a modern Bible translation and create a tune for it, or rewrite the psalm for yourself, with rhyming lines if you wish.
2. Or you could use a familiar tune that everyone knows, such as the theme tune from a TV program and then create a song to fit the tune.
3. You can also make up songs without needing to write the music.

Another idea:

- Choose a favorite Bible verse and create a simple tune for it. This can help children to learn their memory verses. Children are often able to make up their own tunes too.

94

Scrapbook of Songs

Choose a selection of songs that inspire you and create your own illustrated album of the words.

THINGS YOU NEED:

- Words for your favorite songs
- Scrapbook or mini-scrapbooking album
- Materials for writing the words and decorating the album pages
- Scissors
- Glue
- Pens

What you do:

1. Write out the words for your favorite songs. You could use a computer to print the words in an attractive way or on special papers.
2. Paste the verses for the songs on different pages, and use pictures, stickers, and embellishments to illustrate the themes in the songs.
3. Add verses of Scripture connected to the themes of the songs.

Other ideas:

- Use this idea to create a scrapbook of any songs that you have written yourself.
- Make a scrapbook of a friend's favorite songs or hymns to give as a gift, or use the hymns and readings from your parents' wedding to create a scrapbook gift for an anniversary gift.

95

Making Your Own Instruments

Making simple rattles to use in family worship can be a fun activity for small children.

THINGS YOU NEED:
- Clean, dry plastic bottles with screw-on lids
- Various dry substances for adding to the bottles such as salt, cornflakes, rice, beans (different substances create different sounds)
- White, water-based adhesive
- Collection of colored papers and other items for decorating the bottles

What you do:
1. Pour one of the dry substances into each of the bottles, screw on the lids, and check the sound that each bottle makes. Adjust the amount if necessary and then screw on the lids tightly, adding glue if you wish, to secure the lid.
2. Decorate the outside of the bottle with colored paper, foil, cellophane, or other decorative materials.
3. Sing some lively praise songs, and let your child shake the bottles in time to the music.

Other ideas:
- Thread bells onto ribbon and tie securely to make jingle bells.
- Fill glass bottles with different amounts of water and tap them with a wooden spoon.
- Find something with an irregular surface that can be scraped with the handle of a wooden spoon to create an interesting sound.
- Explore your home for other things that will make interesting noises and bring them all together to create an improvised praise band.

96

Hymn and Song Stories

Many hymns and songs were written out of interesting life stories. Researching these stories can add to your understanding and appreciation of these songs.

THINGS YOU NEED:
- Hymn and song books
- Books of stories about hymn and song writers
- Album sleeves and booklets that tell stories about why songs were written

What you do:
Research and read all you can about your favorite hymns and songs. When you have found out all you can, you could rewrite the story in your own words. Some stories are available on the Internet on sites such as <www.tanbible. com>.

Other ideas:
- Create mini-dramas based on the background stories of certain hymns.
- Your research could be the basis of a musical church program, combining songs and their stories.

97

Musical Mimes

Miming to Christian praise songs can help the mime artists to appreciate the meaning of the words and to use their whole bodies to praise and worship God.

THINGS YOU NEED:
- CDs or tapes containing songs that inspire actions
- Paper
- Pencils
- Active bodies

What you do:
1. Give everyone a piece of paper and a pencil. As a group, listen to one song several times, jotting down any ideas for mimes and movements as you listen.
2. Discuss your ideas together before creating the mime.
3. Play the music and develop the mime as you practice, so that the movements are smooth and flowing.
4. Perhaps you could find an opportunity to perform this mime at a church program, or maybe you could just enjoy the experience in your own home or group.

Other ideas:
- Divide into small groups, each group choosing a song.
- Practice a mime in the small group and then perform it to the other groups.
- Create your own mime actions for a Bible passage such as the Lord's Prayer or a parable.

98

Sound Scriptures

If you listen to a play on the radio, you will notice how often simple sound effects are used. How might you add sound effects if you were reading from the Scriptures on the radio?

THINGS YOU NEED:

- Bibles
- Pens
- Paper
- A variety of sound makers from around the home or a specialized sound effect CD or tape
- Computer program that has a selection of sound effects that can be inserted into presentations (optional)

What you do:

1. Choose a passage of Scripture that has a variety of sound effects.
2. Read the passage aloud and jot down any ideas you might have for different sound effects.
3. Search for the sound effects, wherever they might be available, or make vocalizations!
4. Enjoy yourselves, **but be careful not to be irreverent!**

Other ideas:

- Record your Scripture and sound effects so that you can listen to how your presentation could be improved.
- Have fun creating your own sound effects for the things mentioned in Psalm 104!
- These sound Scriptures could be used as part of a children's program or other church event.

99

Christian Drama

Reading Christian plays together can be an enjoyable Sabbath activity. If you take the time to rehearse and polish your skills, the dramas could be used in a church program or street witnessing project.

THINGS YOU NEED:

- Scripts for Christian plays from books or from the Internet. Visit <www.fools4christ.co.uk> for free mime scripts and resources for Christian plays. Search the Internet using keywords—Christian scripts, Christian drama, etc.

What you do:

1. Make sure that each person has a copy of the script that you are using.
2. Assign each person a character and give them time to read the script through to themselves a couple of times before trying to read it together.
3. As you become more acquainted with the script, introduce sound effects and acting.

Other ideas:

- Write your own scripts based on Bible stories, stories behind hymns and songs, or biographies of famous Christians.
- Choose a theme and write a sketch that illustrates the theme you have chosen.

Illustrated Songs

Combining songs with visual images can create a powerful and inspiring presentation for use during worship at home or in church.

THINGS YOU NEED:

- A computer with PowerPoint software, or similar
- Extra royalty-free images from Web sites such as <www.gettyimages. com>.

What you do:

1. Create a PowerPoint presentation combining images with the words of the song. Choose images that convey the meaning or feeling of the song where possible. Make the presentation as simple or as complex as your skills allow. Choosing images to match the words can be an inspiring activity.
2. If you work as a group, you could all help to select appropriate images for the song.

Other ideas:

- If your church uses PowerPoint presentations, your final creation could be used in a church service.
- If you don't have access to PowerPoint, select a song and find images in magazines, newspapers, and old calendars to illustrate the words. Or create a series of your own photographs to illustrate the words. These could be made into a scrapbook or a poster.
- Illustrate children's songs with pictures in the place of words to help those who are prereaders or beginning readers.

If you appreciate these as well:

100 Creative Prayer Ideas for Kids

Karen Holford. Do you or your children struggle to know what to say when asked to pray? Is prayer time becoming routine around your house—even boring? Here are 100 creative prayer ideas that are guaranteed to make time with Jesus interesting, meaningful, and even fun.

0-8163-1968-5. Paperback
US$11.99, Can$17.99.

100 Quick and Easy Worship Ideas for Kids

Karen Holford. In the tradition of *100 Creative Prayer Ideas for Kids,* Karen Holford presents *100 Quick and Easy Worship Ideas for Kids,* which will transform your family time with Jesus. Gather the kids around, choose any one of the ideas from this book, and watch what happens as together, you find new ways to experience God.

0-8163-2051-9. Paperback.
US$11.99, Can$17.99.

Daniel Asks About Baptism and Communion

Strange things happen at church sometimes, and little Daniel wants to understand. In this book for children aged five to seven, Heather J. Hanna provides a fully illustrated story to help your child understand, and one day prepare for, baptism and the Communion service.

0-8163-2083-7
US$5.99, Can$8.49

Order from your ABC by calling 1-800-765-6955, or get online and shop our virtual store at <www.AdventistBookCenter.com>.

• Read a chapter from your favorite book
• Order online
• Sign up for email notices on new products